AMERICAN CRUISERS OF WORLD WAR II

A Pictorial Encyclopedia

USS St. Paul (CA-73), the last all-gun cruiser
off Diamond Head, Waikiki Beach, Hawaii circa 1970, USN

By Steve Ewing

PICTORIAL HISTORIES PUBLISHING COMPANY
MISSOULA, MONTANA

COPYRIGHT © 1984 STEVE EWING.

All rights reserved. No part of this book
may be used or reproduced without written
permission of the publisher.

LIBRARY OF CONGRESS
CATALOG CARD NUMBER 84-61620

ISBN 0-933126-51-4

First Printing: November 1984
Second Printing: December 1985
Third Printing: January 1987
Fourth Printing: January 1989
Fifth Printing: February 1991

Typography: Arrow Graphics & Typography
Layout: Stan Cohen
Cover Design: Allen Woodard

OTHER BOOKS BY STEVE EWING

The Lady Lex and the Blue Ghost (1983)

USS ENTERPRISE: The Most Decorated Ship of World War Two (1982)

West Virginia and Appalachia (1977)

Man, Religion and The Environment (1975)

Front cover: USS Northampton (CA-26) off Pearl Harbor
circa 1940. USN

PICTORIAL HISTORIES PUBLISHING COMPANY
713 South Third West
Missoula, Montana 59801

TABLE OF CONTENTS

INTRODUCTION

FROM 7 DECEMBER 1941 UNTIL 2 SEPTEMBER 1945, 74 United States cruisers—two battlecruisers, 25 heavy cruisers and 47 light cruisers—fought in at least one battle against Germany, Japan or both and therefore received recognition by the award of a battle star. This pictorial history is the story of those 74 cruisers with one or more battle stars.

In the nearly 40 years since the end of that great and terrible conflict, journalists have not found it difficult to write about American aircraft carriers, battleships, destroyers and submarines. World War II in the Pacific was a carrier war and consequently there have been many books on carriers. Battleship exploits have been a little more difficult to present because there were only two major victories—*Washington* (BB-56) against *Kirishima* at Guadalcanal in November 1942 and the prewar battleship action at Suriago Strait during the Battle of Leyte Gulf. Nevertheless, the aura of the battleship is as large as the vessels themselves, and even in 1983 the World War II vintage *New Jersey* (BB-62) still commands extraordinary attention. And as long as sea stories are told, the heroic charge of the destroyers *Hoel* and *Johnston* and destroyer-escort *Samuel B. Roberts* at Leyte Gulf will capture the imagination. Submarine narratives, meanwhile, properly emphasize the many victories of the "pigboats" over enemy combatants of all classifications and stress their well-documented statistics concerning the enormous enemy merchant tonnage sunk.

It is not as easy to report the account of cruisers. The reality is that several of their most notable battles were defeats. After Pearl Harbor, major American surface-action defeats primarily involved cruisers and on no occasion did American cruisers score a clear-cut surface victory equal to their defeats at Savo Island in August 1942 or Tassafaronga in November 1942. It has been said that people tend to remember only the very best or worst of things and this may apply to the American public's remembrance of their heavy and light cruisers during World War II. However, there was much between these two extremes for which American cruisers deserve to be remembered. Indeed, when viewed in full, the history of these ships records success and triumph as much as sacrifice and frustration. Cruisers participated in nearly all major surface battles and air-sea battles. Highly adaptable to unforeseen wartime needs, cruisers expanded their functions far beyond original expectations. Before the war was over cruisers had traded broadsides with enemy battleships, had practically steamed onto enemy-held islands to provide close gunfire support, and had even transformed nine of their sisters into aircraft carriers (CVLs).

Heavy with awards and honors at the end of World War II, most of these cruisers rested in reserve for varying periods before being towed off to be broken up. Others, however, continued to serve through the Korean War era and even the Vietnam conflict before also being scrapped. Of the 74 cruisers to win one or more battle stars in World War II, only four cruisers and one light carrier that had been converted from a cruiser hull still existed in early 1982 when research for this book began. The carrier belongs to Spain (*Dedalo*, formerly the *Cabot*), two cruisers belong to Chile (*O'Higgins*—formerly the *Brooklyn*, and *Chacabuco*—previously *Capitan Prat* and *Nashville*), while neither of the two remaining cruisers (*Chicago* and *Okalahoma City*) is on active duty and neither resembles its World War II appearance. Sad to say but no World War II era cruiser has been preserved. Remembrance, therefore, can be sustained only by words and pictures.

PREFACE TO THE SECOND PRINTING

The second printing of *American Cruisers of World War II* includes several changes. The battle star totals listed in the first printing were taken from official Navy sources. However, a few veterans challenged the total for their respective cruisers and in one case a review by the Ships' History Section of the Naval Historical Center resulted in the award of a previously uncounted star. The men of the *USS Minneapolis CA-36* can thank their own Don Bovill and John C. Reilly, Jr. of the Naval Historical Center for the recognition of *CA-36*'s 17th battle star. This recognition ties the *Minneapolis* with *San Francisco* for the highest number of battle stars awarded to cruisers in World War II and also places *CA-36* in a tie for second (behind *Enterprise CV-6*) for most battle stars in all ship classifications. Another challenge on behalf of the *USS New Orleans CA-32* is still pending.

Apologies go to the men of the *USS Portland CA-33*, *USS Marblehead CL-12*, *USS Philadelphia CL-41*, *USS Honolulu CL-48*, *USS St. Louis CL-49* and the *USS Birmingham CL-62* for the omission of their well-deserved Navy Unit Commendations. It must be noted that these awards are also omitted from the *Dictionary of American Naval Fighting Ships*, an official government publication which includes the history of all U.S. Navy ships. This same source also omits an accounting of the exploits of the *USS Detroit CL-8* off Iwo Jima and Okinawa. Still, responsibility of perpetuating these omissions—and any other errors—is the fault of this writer.

New in this printing is a listing on page 140 of all cruisers in World War II that won the Presidential Unit Citation or the Navy Unit Commendation. On the same page is a listing of the 10 cruisers that were lost during the war.

ACKNOWLEDGEMENTS

RESEARCH ASSISTANCE FOR THIS BOOK WAS PROVIDED BY Agnes F. Hoover, C.R. Haberlein, John C. Reilly Jr., and John Vajda of the Naval Historical Center; Marvin Reinhart (USN), W.L. Striegiel (USN), and Tom Walkowiak; and World War II veterans Cmdr. Perry W. Ustick (USN, Ret.), Capt. J.C. Haynie (USN, Ret.), Frank Peigler, Robert Baxter, John Melton, Glen Randolph, Francis Russell, Dutch Lawson, Clarence J. Tibado, Earl Lockard, Fred Chafin, Joe Tokar and Phil Titus.

A special thanks is offered to Jack Sotherland for drawing attention to the fact that no pictorial history was available of U.S. World War II combat-active cruisers and for suggesting a need for such a book. Further inspiration and assistance was rendered by publisher Stan Cohen, Mr. and Mrs. William P. Belcher, Mr. and Mrs. Wilber A. Ewing, Ms. Elizabeth Wright, Dr. Jack Rhodes, Dr. W.B. West Jr., Scott Pohlman, Mrs. Myrle Border, and Capt. John Adams (USN, Ret.).

President Ernest Clevenger Jr. and Academic Dean Dr. Linda Brooks of Faulkner University provided considerable encouragement and support for this project, just as they have for earlier books. Professor Karen Hightower again took time from her academic duties and family to edit the manuscript while Anna Williams, Lisa Cooper, Cynthia Faircloth, Paul Alburl, Marty Rucker and Cole Lang furnished clerical assistance. And, in fairness, it is time to recognize the patience that my students have demonstrated over the years at West Virginia Tech, West Virginia State, the University of Charleston, the University of Southern Mississippi and now Faulkner University. This writer has too often carried the frustrations and joys of research and writing into the classroom.

Finally, appreciation is expressed to Roger Ellenburg for his construction of the two Solomon Islands maps, and to Ron Moreland, director of the Pensacola Naval Air Station Library, for his research in compiling the sources listed in the bibliography. These sources were valuable not only for this book but also for students of naval history who wish to know more about World War II cruisers.

NAVY DAY · OCTOBER 27TH
Anniversary of Theodore Roosevelt's Birth

U. S. S. PENSACOLA
In The Panama Canal

334

NRB—14291—10-2-31—18M

"The best possible assurance against war is an adequate Navy." — — Theodore Roosevelt.

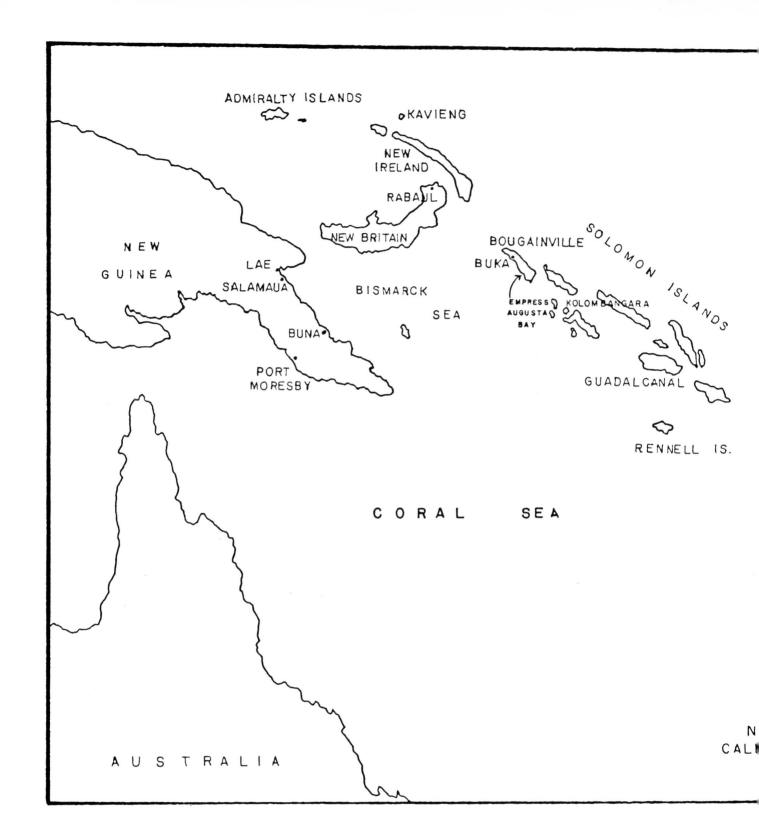

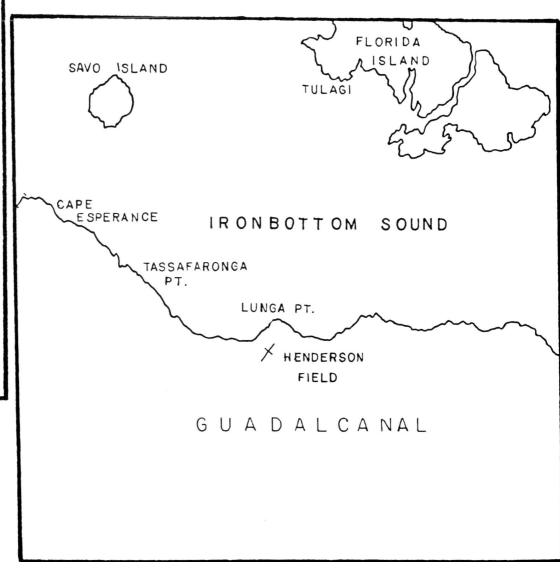

SANTA CRUZ IS.

ESPIRITU SANTO

OUMEA

SAVO ISLAND

FLORIDA ISLAND

TULAGI

CAPE ESPERANCE

IRONBOTTOM SOUND

TASSAFARONGA PT.

LUNGA PT.

HENDERSON FIELD

GUADALCANAL

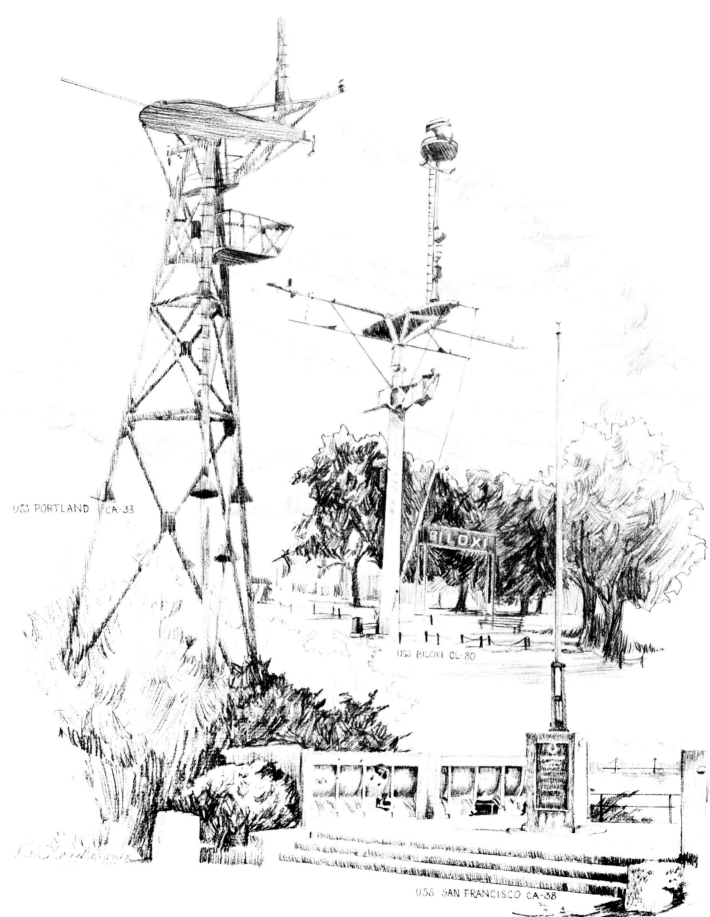

USS PORTLAND CA-33

BILOXI

USS BILOXI CL-80

USS SAN FRANCISCO CA-38

Contemporary cruiser memorials.
by Diane Ewing Buchanan

THE DEVELOPMENT OF
AMERICAN CRUISERS

CRUISERS WERE AN IMPORTANT AND integral part of the United States Navy long before World War II. From the beginning of the American Navy, there was a need for the functions eventually supplied by cruisers. Early sailing ships departed their home ports to scout and probe, to raid enemy commerce along well-established trade routes, and to close with and destroy enemy warships of relatively equal strength. To accomplish the several functions assigned to it, a cruiser had to be fast. It had to bring news of trouble before the trouble arrived, it had to overtake commercial vessels, and it had to possess sufficient speed to run away from larger, more heavily armed and armored ships which it could not outfight.

The coming of World War II did not diminish the early functions of the cruiser. Rather, new functions and expectations were added, as will be seen later in this narrative. But even with the new demands in World War II, the basics of the cruiser changed little. Always the cruiser would be fast. It would for the most part be of medium tonnage, be capable of steaming long distances, possess a minimum of armor protection and carry armament that would allow it to join battle with any warship except a battlewagon. Too, the cruiser would provide an optimum return in terms of versatility and gunpower versus cost. When compared to the construction cost and extended operating expense of a battleship, the cruiser was an enticing bargain.

The terms "heavy cruiser" and "light cruiser" had expression during World War I and the distinction in the use of "heavy" or "light" depended primarily on whether a cruiser was scouting (light) or raiding shipping lanes (heavy). The more precise usage of the terms that would distinguish the two types of cruisers came into being soon after World War I when the Washington Naval Conference convened in November 1921 and the London Conference convened in January 1930. These conferences, inspired by a need for reducing government expenditures as well as a desire for peace, primarily addressed reduction in battleships. Even so, cruisers received meaningful attention.

By early 1922, when the governments of the United States, Great Britain, Japan, France and Italy approved the Washington Naval Treaty, the definition of a heavy cruiser was determined to be a warship not in excess of 10,000 tons with guns not capable of firing shells over 8 inches in diameter. A light cruiser would now be defined as a warship with gun calibers not exceeding 6 inches in diameter. The treaty set the same 5-5-3 ratio (United States, Great Britain and Japan, respectively) for heavy cruisers that was agreed upon for battleships but set no limits for the number of light cruisers that any of the signatories might possess. American delegates, who greatly favored the 8-inch gunned cruiser for potential use in the Pacific, championed the move for the limitation on heavy cruisers, while the British, who were quite sensitive to their need to protect widespread and extensive sea lanes, were the major proponents for an unlimited number of light cruisers.

With their definitions formalized by the Washington Conference, a class of 10 new American cruisers (*Omaha* class) authorized during World War I (1916) and completed after the war's end became "light" cruisers, as their largest guns were 6-inch. Slow, armored cruisers that had been built around the turn of the century technically became heavy cruisers as they carried some 8-inch guns, but many of these cruisers would soon be scrapped in compliance with the treaty or due to obsolescence and none would fight in World War II. Many, however, would pass their names on to newer cruisers that would participate in the 1941-1945 conflict. Consequently, the first true "treaty" heavy cruisers were the two 8-inch gunned cruisers of the *Pensacola* class authorized in 1924.

The limitations agreed upon at Washington in 1922 along with later agreements at London in 1930-1931 resulted in some design constrictions with consequent performance disappointments. Newer construction techniques and design alterations would remedy early problems until the last prewar heavy cruisers authorized in 1940 (*Baltimore* class) were freed from treaty limitations by the withdrawal of Japan in 1936 and the onset of the European war in September 1939. Still, from 1922 until 1939 American cruisers would conform to promises made at the Washington Conference.

The *Pensacola* and *Salt Lake City* were only two of eight ships authorized in 1924. The original legislation called for eight cruisers, but the building of the last six was delayed due to appropriation problems, thanks in part to the conservative fiscal policies of President Calvin Coolidge. To some degree the delay was fortuitous. The *Pensacolas* were deficient in freeboard, rolled heavily at slow speeds and sacrificed a portion of their armor protection in order to carry ten 8-inch guns in four turrets. When the other six ships of the 1924 authorization were built—the *Northampton* class—changes were implemented. The most obvious change in the *Northamptons* was the arrangement of nine 8-inch guns in three turrets. Too, there was an improvement in armor, but until the end of treaty limitations and the design of the *Baltimore* class, all American cruisers were insufficiently armored.

In 1927 legislation was submitted to build 25 cruisers, but final authorization in 1929 called for 15, and when the London Treaty became operational in January 1931, the allowed number for heavy cruisers was reduced to 10. From this building program came the two heavy cruisers of the *Portland* class, the seven heavy cruisers of the *New Orleans* class and the one heavy cruiser of the *Wichita* class. The *Northamptons*, *Portlands*, *New Orleans* and *Wichita*-class cruisers were built between 1928 and 1939 and all were in commission before war broke out in Europe. Along with the earlier *Pensacola* class, each of these ships would see more than their fair share of the coming global conflict.

Although the provisions of the London Treaty went into effect on 1 January 1931, provisions concerning cruisers would soon prove to have little meaning. Limitations within the London Treaty even more precisely distinguished heavy cruisers from light cruisers: a light cruiser could displace a maximum of 10,000 tons, guns could not be more than 6.1 inches, and for the first time there would be aggregate tonnage limitations on light cruisers as well as the heavy cruisers. But before these provisions could meaningfully affect the U.S. Navy, political changes in Japan and Germany would inspire rearmament instead of disarmament. Beginning in 1931, military influence in Japanese political affairs would begin a long series of treaty violations. Of particular significance to naval interests was the appearance in the early 1930s of the Japanese *Mogami*-class cruisers. The *Mogamis* were supposedly light crusers of 8,500 tons. Armed with fifteen 6-inch guns they would be a match for any 8-inch gunned heavy cruiser due to the more rapid rate of fire of their 6-inch guns. In fact, these ships would top out at 12,500 tons and by 1941 they had been modified to carry eight 8-inch guns to become heavy cruisers. Although the variance between the actual and announced figures on these cruisers was not known outside Japan, the U.S. Navy was sufficiently impressed with Japanese claims; a class of cruisers (*Brooklyn* class) was designed and built to meet the potential threat.

By the spring of 1933 Franklin D. Roosevelt had become president and the U.S. Navy could not have asked for a stronger friend in high places. Formerly assistant secretary of the Navy during President Wilson's tenure, Roosevelt quickly turned attention to the Navy he loved so dearly. Accomplishing several objectives with one action, he allotted $238 million to fight unemployment by providing work in American shipyards and to strengthen the Navy. Funds from Roosevelt's June 1933 grant, along with funds from the 1934 Vinson-Trammell Act, built the seven ships of the *Brooklyn* class. These gave the United States its answer to the Japanese *Mogamis* and they were the country's first modern light cruisers since the completion of the *Omaha* class in January 1925. The Vinson-Trammell Act also was the authorization for the two light cruisers of the *Helena* class.

By late 1939 and early 1940, problems in the Far East and Europe were such that Congress soon passed the Naval Expansion Act and the Two-Ocean Navy Bill. These pre-Pearl Harbor programs authorized the *Atlanta*-class anti-aircraft light cruisers, the *Cleveland*-class light cruisers, the *Baltimore*-class heavy cruisers and the *Alaska*-class battlecruisers. Not all of the cruisers authorized in these last four classes would be complete in time to participate in World War II.

In general it can be stated that the later heavy cruisers were indeed heavier, better protected with armor, slightly faster and had a greater range. Most of the later light cruisers displaced the same tonnage as the heavy cruisers described in the treaty and mounted fewer main armament 6-inch guns. And as World War II progressed, all cruisers added medium and light anti-aircraft guns in every available topside location along with added gun directors and updated radar installations.

During World War II, cruisers were still utilized for raiding (mostly tracking German raiders), scouting (particularly with their planes), battling enemy surface forces and serving as flagships. Additionally, cruisers filled new and important roles in defending carriers from air attack and in supporting amphibious operations by providing fire support close inshore.

Forty years after World War II the cruiser still commands a major position in the U.S. Navy. Though the 8-inch and 6-inch guns are gone, missiles and rapid-fire smaller caliber weapons give the present-day cruiser a punch her World War II ancestors would envy.

HEAVY
CRUISERS

HEAVY CRUISERS

THE 18 PREWAR "TREATY" CRUISERS REPAID the taxpayer many times over in service to the country. All won battle stars, all suffered damage and casualties, and seven of the 18 (39 percent) were lost as a result of battle damage. The *Baltimore*-class heavy cruisers were not available until after the Pacific war began, but seven of the class won battle stars and proved especially useful in the final stages of the war when the Navy closed on the shores of Japanese island possessions as well as on the home islands themselves. None of the *Baltimores* were lost and the damage they incurred was relatively light. As fate would have it, only the prewar "treaty" heavy cruisers would engage in the surface battles of 1942 and 1943. The *Baltimores* arrived after the character of the war had changed and fleet battles became almost exclusively air-sea battles.

In the first year of the war American heavy cruisers assumed a primary role that in prewar thinking would have been served by battleships. After Pearl Harbor, heavy cruisers—and light cruisers, for that matter—found themselves in the first line of surface defense even when it meant facing Japanese battleships. This did not occur often, and at war's end the American heavy cruisers' biggest problem had proved to be fast-running, long-lance torpedoes launched by Japanese destroyers. Throughout the war, however, the heavy cruisers fulfilled all the functions mentioned earlier and were invaluable in both the Pacific and Atlantic theaters.

The basic configuration of American heavy cruisers was stable throughout World War II, but there were constant minor changes as new electronic devices and anti-aircraft guns were added. Tripod masts were often removed and pole masts installed to reduce topside weight as well as make room for light anti-aircraft weapons and improve the arc of anti-aircraft guns.

Pensacola, Salt Lake City and *New Orleans* at Pearl Harbor in 1943.   NA

Many prewar heavy cruisers were built to accommodate flag officers and their staffs. Here, *Indianapolis* hosts dignitaries as the three *Maryland*-class battleships *(Maryland, West Virginia* and *Colorado)* pass in review.　　NA

Minneapolis, Wichita, Chester and *New Orleans* in mothballs at the Philadelphia Navy Yard in the 1950s. Regrettably, no battle-active World War II cruiser was retained as a memorial ship. The few cruisers of the era still in the United States that are not yet dismantled no longer possess their World War II configuration.　　USN

THE PENSACOLA CLASS

THE TWO MEMBERS OF THIS CLASS, *PENSACOLA* (CA-24) and *Salt Lake City* (CA-25), were the first two cruisers to be built in compliance with the 1922 Washington Naval Treaty. During World War II each compiled a distinguished record, with *Pensacola* earning 13 battle stars and *Salt Lake City* 11. *Salt Lake City* was also awarded the Navy Unit Commendation for her performance in the Aleutian Campaign.

The *Pensacolas* were authorized by Congress in the December 1924 act at a cost of approximately $8.5 million each. The complement of each ship was 700 officers and men in peacetime, and approached 1,200 during the war. Both ships were designed to be 585 feet in overall length, have a beam of 65 feet, displace 9,100 tons standard (13,100 tons in war service) and possess a draft of 15 feet when empty and 22 feet when loaded. Top speed on trials for both vessels was over 32 knots. The ships had 107,000 horsepower, four shafts, carried 3,088 tons of fuel and had a cruising radius of 10,100 miles at 15 knots or 4,400 miles at 25 knots.

Protection for the *Pensacola* and *Salt Lake City* was light by later standards. The two heavy cruisers had only a 3-inch side-armor belt, 2-inch plus 1-inch deck armor and only 1.5-inch turret side protection. The relative paucity of armor protection is apparent when these figures are compared with those of the *Baltimore* class, which possessed up to 6 inches of side armor and 3 plus 2 inches of deck armor. Five to 6 inches on turret faces was standard for all heavy-cruiser classes.

For their function as combat vessels, CA-24 and CA-25 carried four scout planes which could be launched from either of two catapults located amidships. The main armament was ten 8-inch guns in four turrets, two fore and two aft with triple top turrets and dual lower turrets. This design would be unique as future heavy cruisers would mount nine 8-inch guns in triple turrets, two forward and one aft. Originally the two ships carried four 5-inch guns, but this was increased to eight during the war. The original design provided for six 21-inch torpedo tubes but these were removed prior to the attack on Pearl Harbor. Early anti-aircraft guns, .50-caliber machine guns and 1.1-inch quads were replaced in 1942 by the standard light and medium anti-aircraft guns of the war—the 20mm Oerlikons and 40mm Bofors.

The *Pensacolas* suffered from several design and construction problems. Although most problems were satisfactorily rectified early on, the ships had a major vibration problem, rolled badly at slow speed and had defective sternposts. As wartime demands for topside space increased to accommodate newer and heavier anti-aircraft guns in addition to radar and gun directors, and as more berthing space was needed, some weight was saved by the removal of the tripod mainmast and its replacement with a pole.

PENSACOLA CA-24

(13 Battle Stars) Named for a port city in northwest Florida and the location of the U.S. Navy's home of naval aviation training, *Pensacola* (CA-24) was laid down at the New York Navy Yard 27 October 1926. She was sponsored at her launch by Mrs. Joseph L. Seligman on 25 April 1929 and was commissioned 6 February 1930 with Capt. Alfred F. Howe as her first commanding officer.

From 1930 to 1934 *Pensacola* operated mostly in the Atlantic. In January 1935 she joined the Pacific Fleet, with her home port in San Diego, and then moved to Pearl Harbor in October 1939 just after war began in Europe.

When the Japanese attacked Pearl Harbor on 7 December 1941, *Pensacola* was at sea with a convoy en route to the ill-fated Philippines, but news of the attack diverted the ships to Australia. Returning quickly to Pearl, she helped patrol the area between Pearl and Samoa. In February 1942 she joined a task force built around the *Lexington* (CV-2) and saw her first action when the task force was unsuccessfully attacked near Bougainville in the Solomon Islands. In June 1942 *Pensacola* participated in the Battle of Midway as part of the

Enterprise (CV-6) screen and returned to Midway two weeks after the battle to bring Marine reinforcements to that key outpost.

In August 1942 the United States began the long trek across the Pacific by invading Guadalcanal in the southeastern Solomon Islands. In the ensuing months *Pensacola* would see considerable action. On 26 October 1942 *Pensacola* was in the screen that attempted to defend the carrier *Hornet* (CV-8) during the Battle of Santa Cruz. In one of the heaviest Japanese air attacks of the war, the *Hornet* was fatally damaged, but the combination of damage to enemy carriers by *Hornet* and *Enterprise* air groups, the low fuel reserves in Japanese ships, and the presence of *Pensacola* and other American surface units, helped turn back this second of the three major enemy fleet efforts to reinforce Guadalcanal.

Pensacola returned to Noumea, New Caledonia, long enough to drop off nearly 200 survivors from the *Hornet* and then returned to the waters around Guadalcanal to land troops and supplies—a function not originally perceived for heavy cruisers—and helped screen the U.S. Navy's last operational carrier in the Pacific, the *Enter-*

First of the "treaty" cruisers, *Pensacola*, shown here in the early 1930s, was distinct from later heavy cruisers by carrying four turrets with a total of ten 8-inch guns. Note the torpedo tubes, later removed, outboard of the aft stack.

USN

prise, during the decisive Naval Battle of Guadalcanal on 12-13 November 1942.

As a member of cruiser-destroyer Task Force 67, *Pensacola* participated in the infamous Battle of Tassafaronga (more fully described under *Northampton*) on 29-30 November 1942. Steaming to intercept Japanese destroyers and transports attempting to supply the Guadalcanal garrison, *Pensacola* was caught in the spread of torpedoes that disabled *Minneapolis* and *New Orleans* and sank *Northampton*. Turning to port to avoid the two damaged heavy cruisers in front of her, *Pensacola* ran into the track of a long-lance torpedo. The torpedo struck directly below the mainmast on the port side.

Although water engulfed one engine room and three of the four 8-inch turrets lost power, the major problem was fire. Ruptured oil tanks fed the fire covering the rear quarter of the ship and exploding ammunition added to the problems of damage control. Not until noon on the 30th were the last fires extinguished. Total casualties were 125 killed and 68 wounded, a far greater toll than was exacted from the lost *Northampton*. After initial repairs in Tulagi Harbor, *Pensacola* sailed to Espiritu Santo in December and from there made the journey to Pearl Harbor to begin repairs that would keep her out of the war for nearly all of 1943.

In November 1943 *Pensacola* returned to combat fully repaired and carrying numerous new 40mm and 20mm anti-aircraft guns. The new guns would be needed as the cruiser stepped into the primary role of anti-aircraft defense for the fast-growing number of new carriers that were arriving from American shipyards to spearhead the offensive across the Pacific. During the early conquests of the Marshall and Gilbert islands in the winter of 1943, *Pensacola* served in carrier screens and trained her 8-inch guns on Betio, Tarawa, Tarao, Wotje and Maloelap Atoll. In the spring the cruiser screened carriers raiding the Caroline Islands before departing to the Northern Pacific. From June through early August she was in action in the Kuriles where her shellings helped convince the Japanese to evacuate the region.

On her way back to the central Pacific, *Pensacola* participated in the shelling of Wake Island on 3 September and the bombardment of Marcus Island on 9 October. In the following weeks *Pensacola* screened carriers and provided gunfire support in the Philippine Campaign. The cruiser participated in the Leyte invasion and the "baited" Cape Engano battle. On 12 November 1944 and 8 December 1944 the cruiser shelled Iwo Jima and returned to Iwo on 16 February as part of a battleship-cruiser bombardment force to support the invasion. On 17 February the ferocity of the fight for Iwo came home to *Pensacola* as she took six hits from enemy shore batteries and suffered casualties of 17 killed and 119 wounded. The cruiser was away from her assigned duties of covering minesweepers close inshore for only a short period to make repairs and she remained off Iwo until 3

Pensacola with the wounded *Yorktown* (CV-5) at Midway. Detached from the *Enterprise* screen, *Pensacola* added her anti-aircraft firepower to the defense of the ill-fated carrier.   NA

With main batteries pointing toward Iwo Jima, *Pensacola* pounds enemy positions. On 17 February 1945 the cruiser suffered casualties of 17 killed and 119 wounded as a result of taking six shells from Japanese guns.   USN

March. On 25 March *Pensacola* began her last battle as she supported the Okinawa operation preliminaries. As cruisers could move closer to shore than battleships, *Pensacola* again used her guns to cover minesweepers. After providing gunfire support for the invasion from 1 April to 15 April, the cruiser departed for San Francisco to undergo overhaul.

When the war ended *Pensacola* was at sea off Alaska. After sailing to Japan she then steamed to Iwo to pick up troops and from there she went on to Pearl, San Francisco, and back to the Pacific (Guam) for more troops. Finally, in January 1946 she arrived at San Diego.

The final chapter in the life of *Pensacola* was somewhat protracted. Along with sister ship *Salt Lake City*, carrier *Saratoga*, U.S. battleships *Nevada*, *Pennsylvania*, *Arkansas*, *New York*, the Japanese battleship *Nagato* and light cruiser *Sakawa*, the German heavy cruiser *Prinz Eugen* and approximately 90 other ships, *Pensacola* would be part of Operation Crossroads, the atom bomb experiments at Bikini Atoll. On 1 July 1946 a 20-kiloton atomic bomb was dropped by a B-29. Several ships near the blast sank quickly. In test "Able" *Pensacola* lost both stacks, had her boilers ruined and her superstructure badly damaged, but she did not sink. On 25 July 1946 the cruiser endured test *Baker*, an underwater 50-kiloton atomic blast that sank *Saratoga*, *Arkansas* and *Nagato*. Too radioactive to preserve or return to the fleet, *Pensacola* was decommissioned on 26 August 1946 and after further radiological studies she was sunk as a target ship approximately 100 miles off the coast of Washington on 10 November 1948.

Close-up view of *Pensacola's* forward stack and mast after surviving the atom bomb blasts in the summer of 1946. NA

Pensacola is straddled by shells from the guns of U.S. Navy ships 10 November 1948 off the coast of Washington.

USN

With her bow and stern blown off, *Pensacola* begins the final voyage to the bottom 10 November 1948.　　　USN

SALT LAKE CITY CA-25

(**11 Battle Stars, Naval Unit Commendation**) Named for the capital of Utah, this ship was laid down at the New York Shipbuilding Co. of Camden, N.J., on 9 June 1927. She was sponsored at her launch on 23 January 1929 by Miss Helen Budge and was commissioned on 11 December 1929 with Capt. F.L. Oliver commanding.

After completing shakedown trials in the winter of 1930 *Salt Lake City* spent her first two years operating in the North and South Atlantic. However, from 1932 to the beginning of the war she spent the vast majority of her time in the Pacific, particularly San Pedro, Calif. Had not a storm and a fueling mishap aboard *Northampton* occurred during the first week of December 1941, *Salt Lake City* would have been in Pearl Harbor during the Sunday morning attack. As it was, *Salt Lake City* was one of three cruisers and several destroyers with the carrier *Enterprise* 200 miles west of Pearl Harbor on that fateful Sunday morning. The storm that covered the track of the approaching Japanese raiding force also beat upon the American ships that were returning from a delivery of planes to Wake Island. The storm was sufficiently rough to cause damage to two American destroyers and consequently word was passed from Admiral Halsey to reduce speed. While the drop in speed brought relief to sailors on the destroyers it brought consternation to the men on the *Enterprise* and cruisers as it meant the loss of liberty on Saturday evening in Hawaii.

For the dark early months of the war *Salt Lake City* remained in the force built around *Enterprise.* Consequently, she was in the screen when the first raids against enemy territory were recorded in the Marshalls, at Marcus Island, and in the Halsey-Doolittle Tokyo raid. During the February 1942 Marshall Islands raid *Salt Lake City* joined *Northampton* and *Chester* in shore bombardment and then helped fight off the retaliatory air strikes. Still with *Enterprise* in May, she was one day too late for the Battle of the Coral Sea. When the three *Yorktown* class carriers—*Yorktown, Enterprise* and *Hornet*—steamed to Midway in early June 1942, *Salt Lake City* was left behind to serve as part of the last line of defense if the carriers failed to stop the Japanese in the pivotal battle of the war.

Arrival in the Solomons in August 1942 put *Salt Lake*

Salt Lake City is followed by *Louisville, Northampton, Pensacola* and other cruisers during training in 1932. USN

The guns of *Salt Lake City* pour shells onto Wake Island 24 February 1942.   USN

City back in the thick of the fighting. Assigned to the protective screen for the carrier *Wasp* (CV-7), *Salt Lake City* was with the carrier when the carrier was sunk by submarine torpedoes on 15 September and she took on board many survivors. On the evening of 11-12 October 1942 *Salt Lake City*, with *San Francisco* (CA-38) and light cruisers *Helena* and *Boise*, engaged in the Battle of Cape Esperance. Of all the surface battles around Guadalcanal only this battle was a clear American tactical victory, although the action was confused from beginning to end. Strategically the battle was a draw as both sides were able to reinforce their garrisons on the embattled island.

The Japanese plan was to send a supply and reinforcement convoy, mostly destroyers, to northwestern Guadalcanal. On the 11th this high-speed convoy was spotted by an American plane. This set in motion Rear Adm. Norman Scott's four cruisers and five destroyers toward interception. Unknown to Scott, a second Japanese force consisting of three cruisers and 22 destroyers commanded by Rear Adm. Aritomo Goto was approximately 50 miles behind the convoy. Its purpose was to cover the transports.

Japanese intelligence reports promised no American units would be in the area; therefore, when a flare set fire to a *Salt Lake City* plane, Admiral Goto's staff believed it

was a signal from the convoy and began signaling via blinker light. Radar on *Helena* picked up Goto's covering force and soon thereafter asked permission of the flagship (*San Francisco*) to fire. A misunderstood reply ("Roger," meaning "message received" was misinterpreted to mean "commence firing.") caused *Helena* to start the shooting. The Japanese ships held return fire because it was believed the shelling was coming from Japanese destroyers in the transport column. Even though both sides eventually realized they had some of their own ships in the line of fire, both turned full fury toward each other. After 30 minutes Goto's column was retreating to the northwest minus the sinking cruiser *Furutaka* and destroyer *Fubuki*. Flagship *Aoba*, carrying the mortally wounded Admiral Goto, was badly damaged. On the American side destroyer *Duncan* was sinking, probably hit by gunfire from American cruisers, *Boise* was severely damaged by Japanese salvos, *Salt Lake City* had taken three major-caliber shells, and destroyer *Farenholt*, also probably hit by American shells, was damaged.

Along with *Boise*, *Salt Lake City* left the Solomons for repairs after the Battle of Cape Esperance. In March 1943 *Salt Lake City* left Pearl and headed for the Aleutians. Her new paint, covering the scars of the previous October, was barely dry before the cruiser was in another tough

Salt Lake City is seen here toward the end of the three-hour Battle of the Komandorski Islands. Hit several times, the cruiser and attending ships were making smoke when this picture was taken.   NA

This picture of a painting by I.R. Lloyd commemorates the furious Battle of the Komandorski Islands 26 March 1943. *Salt Lake City* is seen in the upper right portion of the painting.   USN

fight. On 26 March 1943 a Japanese force of two heavy cruisers, two light cruisers and five destroyers was escorting several heavily laden transports to bases on Attu and Kiska when the ships encountered an American force consisting of one heavy cruiser (*Salt Lake City*), one light cruiser (*Richmond*) and four destroyers. Despite being heavily outgunned, the American force, under Rear Adm. Charles McMorris on the *Richmond*, attacked. For three hours the Battle of the Komandorski Islands raged, and, despite being fought in daylight, only a very small percentage of the several thousand major-caliber shells fired by both sides scored hits. But those that did damaged *Salt Lake City* more than any other. Understandably, the only heavy cruiser in the American formation would be the center of attention. Near the end of the battle the several hits on *Salt Lake City* took their toll and the cruiser came to a stop. Salvation occurred when accompanying destroyers charged the enemy formation after first laying smoke to protect the lifeless heavy cruiser. This destroyer torpedo attack disrupted the Japanese concentration of gunfire against *Salt Lake City* and provided time to start the cruiser moving again. At this point the Japanese commander, Vice Adm. Moshiro Hosogaya, broke off the attack and joined his transports in retreat.

Strategically, the American force was victorious because the Japanese were unable to deliver their supplies to garrisons greatly in need, in addition to the fact that the small American force survived. The battle was more a Japanese loss than American victory considering the premature departure of Hosogaya's ships. Low on fuel and ammunition and fearing an air attack, Admiral Hosogaya retreated just as victory was within his grasp. For her role in the Aleutians *Salt Lake City* was awarded the Navy Unit Commendation.

After the Battle of Cape Esperance and the Battle of the Komandorski Islands, life was somewhat quieter for the *Salt Lake City*. Often in company with sister ship *Pensacola*, *Salt Lake City* supported the invasions of the Marshalls, Gilberts, Carolines, Iwo Jima and Okinawa. And, like her sister ship, she withstood the two atomic blasts at Bikini in July 1946. Decommissioned on 29 August 1946, *Salt Lake City* was sunk as a target 130 miles off the coast of Southern California on 25 May 1948.

Salt Lake City capsizing after being used as a target, June 1948.　　　　　　USN

THE NORTHAMPTON
CLASS

THE SIX MEMBERS OF THIS CLASS—*NORTHAMPTON* (CA-26), *Chester* (CA-27), *Louisville* (CA-28), *Chicago* (CA-29), *Houston* (CA-30) and *Augusta* (CA-31)—were authorized in the same 1924 legislation that authorized *Pensacola* and *Salt Lake City*, but construction of the six *Northamptons* was delayed by President Coolidge until 1927. Built in five different shipyards, all six were designed in accordance with the restrictions agreed to at the Washington Naval Conference.

Like the two *Pensacolas*, the *Northamptons* would see considerable action during World War II. *Louisville* earned 13 battle stars, *Chester* 11, *Northampton* 6, *Chicago* 3 and *Augusta* 3. *Houston* won only 2 battle stars, but after the war when her full story became known she was awarded the Presidential Unit Citation for her heroic fight in the Java Sea. Three of the cruisers in this class were lost as a result of battle damage: class leader *Northampton* at Tassafaronga, *Houston* in the Java Sea and *Chicago* off Rennell Island.

Costing approximately $9 million each, the *Northamptons* maintained a complement of nearly 700 officers and men during peacetime and over 1,200 during the war. The six ships of this class were 15 feet longer than the *Pensacolas* at 600 feet overall, and they featured a forecastle deck. Beam dimensions were nearly the same as the *Pensacolas* at 66 feet, displacement similar at 9,050 tons for *Northampton*, and up to 9,300 for *Chicago*, *Houston* and *Augusta*, while draft measurements were 16 feet average and 23 feet maximum. Top speed for these cruisers exceeded 32 knots on trials. Horsepower was 107,000, and each ship had four shafts, carried 1,500 tons of fuel and had a cruising radius of 10,200 miles at 15 knots or 4,800 miles at 25 knots. Speed, horsepower, number of shafts, fuel capacity and cruising radius were the same as for the *Pensacola* class.

Like the *Pensacolas*, the *Northamptons'* protection was relatively light. Side armor was 3 inches, deck armor 2 inches plus one inch and turrets had one and one-half inch protection on the sides and 5 inches on the turret faces.

Design specifications called for the *Northamptons* to carry four float planes to be launched from two catapults located amidships. Main armament was 8-inch guns but on the *Northamptons* and all future heavy cruisers there would be nine 8-inch guns in three turrets—two forward and one aft. Original design placed four 5-inch guns aboard but the number was increased to 8 during the war. As with the *Pensacolas*, the original design called for six 21-inch torpedo tubes but these were removed in the 1930s. Anti-aircraft protection followed the same pattern as in most prewar ships: .50-caliber machine guns were eventually replaced by 20mm Oerkions and later 1.1-inch quads would be replaced after 1942 with 40mm duals or quads.

Numerous benefits accrued to the *Northamptons* because of their delay in construction, as defects in the *Pensacola* design were addressed. The addition of the forecastle deck was made possible because the ships were below treaty limitations by nearly 900 tons; the added length was welcome to improve seakeeping. Additional weight was saved in the *Northamptons* by regrouping the 8-inch guns in three turrets instead of four. The vibration problem in the *Pensacolas* was resolved in the *Northamptons* by strengthening the hull, but a low center of gravity caused a roll at slow speeds until larger bilge keels were fitted.

The last three units of this class—*Chicago, Houston* and *Augusta*—were given extra space so they could serve as flagships. Indeed, *Augusta* gained the major portion of her fame by carrying President Roosevelt and other ranking officials to wartime conferences. In appearance the *Northamptons* greatly resembled the *Pensacolas* but were easily distinguished by the difference in number of turrets and the pronounced aircraft hangars of the *Northamptons*.

NORTHAMPTON CA-26

(6 Battle Stars) Named for the city in Massachusetts—and not without coincidence the home of President Coolidge—*Northampton* (CA-26) was laid down 12 April 1928 by Bethlehem Steel Corp. in Quincy, Mass. She was sponsored at her launching ceremony 5 September 1929 by Mrs. Calvin Coolidge and was commissioned 17 May 1930 with Capt. Walter N. Vernou commanding.

After her shakedown cruise to the Mediterranean in 1930, *Northampton* trained in the Caribbean before moving to the Pacific in 1932 to her home port of San Pedro. In late 1939 she joined the major units of the fleet in the move to Pearl Harbor and was with *Enterprise, Salt Lake City* and *Chester* 200 miles west of Hawaii when the Japanese attacked. On 1 February 1942 *Northampton* teamed with *Salt Lake City* to bombard Wotje and on 24 February she trained her guns at enemy positions on Wake Island. On 4 March the cruiser steamed off Marcus Island, only 1,000 miles from Japan, while screening *Enterprise*. In April the *Enterprise* group containing the *Northampton* joined with the new *Hornet* to escort Lt. Col. Doolittle's bombers to their launch

Northampton entering the river at Brisbane, Australia, 5 August 1941. Note bow-wave camouflage.   USN

against Tokyo and other enemy targets. Nearly always at the side of *Enterprise*, World War II's most decorated warship, *Northampton* was in the force that arrived one day too late to fight in the Battle of the Coral Sea. After a quick resupply at Pearl she was off again to screen the *Enterprise* at the Battle of Midway in June 1942.

In August *Northampton* steamed toward Guadalcanal. On 15 September she was in a column that came under attack by Japanese submarines. Her sailors watched carrier *Wasp* die and saw battleship *North Carolina* and destroyer *O'Brien* absorb severe damage. Joining carrier *Hornet* during attacks on Bougainville on 5 October, *Northampton* remained with that carrier until the Battle of Santa Cruz on 26 October when *Hornet* was fatally damaged by bombs and torpedoes. Although too badly damaged to continue the fight, *Hornet* was still seaworthy and *Northampton* attempted to tow the carrier to safety while continuing to provide anti-aircraft coverage. Continued air attacks, however, jeopardized not only *Hornet* but also the now slowly moving *Northampton*. Finally the approach of darkness and an enemy surface force necessitated the scuttling of the U.S. Navy's newest carrier. For much of the remainder of the month that she had to live, *Northampton* rejoined the screen of her old friend *Enterprise*, now battered and leaking and the last American carrier in the Pacific.

On 30 November *Northampton* joined heavy cruisers *Minneapolis*, *New Orleans* and *Pensacola*, light cruiser *Honolulu* and six destroyers to intercept eight Japanese destroyer-transports. Under the command of Rear Adm. Raizo Tanaka, the destroyers were attempting to carry troops and supplies to Guadalcanal. The American force, commanded by Rear Adm. C.H. Wright, knew the enemy column was underway. With this advantage, as well as a definite plan of battle, more warships and a big edge in gunpower, a favorable outcome seemed assured in the forthcoming Battle of Tassafaronga.

Discovering the enemy by radar a few minutes before midnight, the American destroyers, as planned, unleashed torpedoes. All missed and their wakes alerted the radarless Japanese to the American presence. Still the advantage was with the American column as the cruisers began firing at the enemy. For nearly seven minutes only American warships were shooting. Following textbook tactics, the Japanese destroyers held their fire, ranged on the flashing guns of American ships (flashless powder for American surface units could have rewritten the history of the Solomons Campaign), aimed, and fired torpedoes.

In these first minutes of battle one enemy destroyer was being pounded and would not see the light of another day, but the Japanese torpedoes were on their way. At 2327 hours the character of the conflict changed radically.

Lead cruiser *Minneapolis* took two torpedoes that dropped the entire forward section of the cruiser in front of her number one turret. *New Orleans*, immediately behind the flagship, veered to miss her sister ship and ran into the track of another torpedo which took off the forward portion of the ship all the way back to the number two turret. *Pensacola*, next in line, also veered to miss the two wounded cruisers and she too was hit on the port quarter. *Honolulu* took no hits but shortly thereafter *Northampton* took two torpedoes on the port quarter. With her forward and aft damage-control parties separated, the area around her mainmast burning fiercely, and water pouring into the ship from the gaping holes, *Northampton* was in serious trouble. Three hours later the flood of water could not be controlled and the cruiser was sinking by the stern. Surprisingly, the death toll was only 49 with 29 wounded.

Although there is never comfort in the loss of a ship that has been a home as well as a bond of pride between men, there was some consolation in the fact that the enemy troops and supplies intended for Guadalcanal did not arrive. Too, most of the crew members of this fighting ship were saved and they helped form the nucleus of the crews for the new battleship *Iowa* and the new heavy cruiser *Boston*.

When the survivors of the *Northampton* meet at their reunions there will always be a significant number of men present from the renowned destroyer *Fletcher* (DD-445). It was the *Fletcher* that came to the rescue of the *Northampton's* men while they were treading water. And at these reunions old *Northampton* men still speak ill of light cruiser *Honolulu* for not stopping to help. Official records indicate *Honolulu* was ordered to search for the enemy and continue the battle rather than engage in rescue operations. Even so, to *Northampton* survivors *Honolulu* will never be forgiven for plowing through and away from them.

View of port side 5-inch guns on *Northampton* in action against Wotje Atoll in the Marshall Islands 1 February 1942.

USN

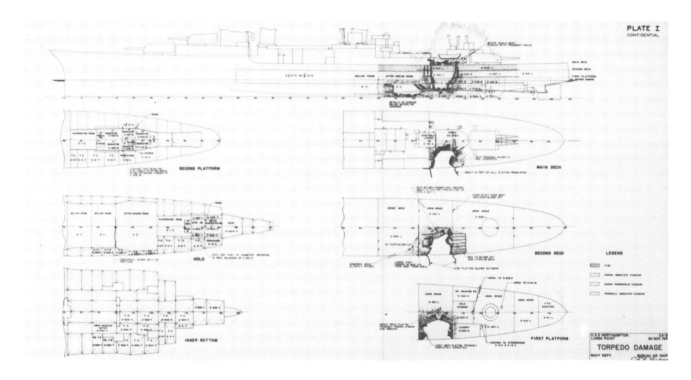

This Bureau of Ships chart shows the fatal torpedo damage suffered by *Northampton* on 30 November 1942. Extensive studies were completed after sinkings to determine, in part, better damage-control techniques.   NA

CHESTER CA-27

(11 Battle Stars) Honoring the city in eastern Pennsylvania, *Chester* (CA-27) was laid down 6 March 1928 by the New York Shipbuilding Co. of Camden, N.J. She was sponsored at her launch on 3 July 1929 by Miss J.T. Blain and was commissioned 24 June 1930 with Capt. A.P. Fairfield commanding. In the 11 years prior to World War II *Chester* steamed extensively in the Atlantic and Pacific with notable cruises to the Mediterranean in 1930, the Philippines in 1935 and South America in 1936. Assigned to Pearl Harbor in February 1941, the cruiser escorted some of the last transports to carry U.S. Army troops to the Philippines in November 1941. Later that month she sailed with sister ship *Northampton* and other warships screening *Enterprise* during the carrier's run to carry planes to Wake Island and was only hours away from Pearl during the infamous attack.

Chester's first direct combat occurred on 1 February 1942. As a member of the group under the command of Admiral Halsey, *Chester* joined in the first offensive raid of the war when she trained her guns on Taroa in the Marshall Islands. During the bombardment *Chester* came under attack by enemy planes and one direct bomb hit killed eight and caused moderate damage.

By late spring 1942 *Chester* was in action screening *Lex-* *ington* (CV-2) and *Yorktown* (CV-5) for the Guadalcanal-Tulagi raid on 4 May, the attack on Misima Island on 7 May and the famous Battle of the Coral Sea on 8 May. *Chester* missed the Battle of Midway in June and the initial landings on Guadalcanal in August due to overhaul, but the cruiser was back in the South Pacific as part of TF 62 for the 2-4 October 1942 landings on Funafuti in the Ellice Islands. But shortly after, on 20 October, the cruiser was steaming southeast of Guadalcanal and she was struck by a submarine torpedo amidships on the starboard side. Eleven men were killed and the cruiser, although able to continue under her own power, was sufficiently crippled and in need of other maintenance that she would miss nearly a year of combat duty.

After a lengthy overhaul at Norfolk, Va., *Chester* participated in the November 1943 Marshall Islands operation, once again bombarding Taroa and new targets on Wotje and Maloelap. In the Marshalls until late April 1944, *Chester* briefly joined TF 94 for a bombardment raid in the Kuriles in June, steamed with TF 12 for the Wake Island raid in September, the Marcus Island raid in October and later the same month she joined TF 38 for the Philippine invasion. Toward the end of 1944 and early months of 1945 *Chester* provided gunfire support and anti-aircraft defense for operations at Iwo Jima. Missing most of the Okinawa campaign for overhaul, the cruiser returned in June 1945 to patrol off Okinawa and support operations off the Chinese coast.

After the war *Chester* made two voyages to carry troops from the Pacific to the United States. Placed out of commission 10 July 1946, the ship was sold for scrap 11 August 1959.

Chester leads *Salt Lake City, Pensacola* and *Northampton* in Panama Bay 21 April 1933 during Fleet Problem 15.   USN

Chester awaits assistance by tugs as she prepares to tie up behind *Indianapolis* at Rio de Janeiro 27 November 1936. This was the first stop of President Franklin D. Roosevelt's "Good Neighbor" cruise to South America.   USN

Taken 16 September 1943 at the Mare Island Navy Yard, this picture provides a good close-up view of the new 40mm anti-aircraft guns and the original 5-inch 25 caliber guns aboard *Chester*.   USN

LOUISVILLE CA-28

(13 Battle Stars) Named for the city in Western Kentucky, *Louisville* (CA-28) was laid down 4 July 1928 at the Puget Sound Navy Yard in Bremerton, Wash. She was sponsored at her launch 1 September 1930 by Miss Jane B. Kennedy and was commissioned 15 January 1931 with Capt. E.J. Marquart in command. Like other prewar cruisers, *Louisville* steamed extensively in both the Atlantic and Pacific, showed the flag, and trained. And not unlike other warships, *Louisville* found excitement and opportunities for service before the onset of war. While in Sydney, Australia, in 1938, crewmen from *Louisville* saved the lives of numerous passengers of a ferryboat that capsized when sightseers overcrowded one side of the vessel to view the American cruiser. And, soon after the European war began in September 1939, *Louisville* steamed through waters made dangerous by lurking German submarines to carry nearly $150 million of British gold from South Africa to New York City.

When war finally embraced the United States, *Louisville* was at sea in the South Pacific. Her first combat came while screening carrier *Yorktown* in the Marshalls-Gilberts raids in February 1942 at which time she lost a scout plane. In June 1942 the cruiser provided convoy escort to the Aleutians and bombarded Kiska Island, and in December she steamed to the Solomon Islands to replace her lost sister ship *Northampton*. As part of TF 18, *Louisville* on 29-30 January 1943 was in company with sister ship *Chicago* and *Wichita* (CA-45) during the Battle of Rennell Island (see *Chicago* CA-29 for details of the battle). During this air-sea battle *Louisville* was hit by one aerial torpedo which failed to detonate and averted another only by radical maneuver. After *Chicago* was wounded by two aerial torpedoes, *Louisville* took her

sister ship in tow for nearly 10 hours, but all undamaged ships of the force were ordered away from *Chicago* before the final and fatal attack on that cruiser the afternoon of the 30th.

In April 1943 *Louisville* again entered the Aleutian Islands area and supported the occupation of Attu in May, bombarded Kiska in July and provided escort for convoys for much of the remainder of 1943. In January and February 1944 the cruiser bombarded Wotje, Roi, Namur and Eniwetok. In the early summer of 1944 *Louisville* shelled Saipan, Tinian and Guam in the Marianas, while in the fall her fire rained on Peleliu in the Palaus Islands and in October she pounded enemy positions in the Philippines. During the Philippines operation *Louisville* was one of the cruisers which, with several veteran battleships, engaged in the Battle of Surigao Strait, the last major surface action of the war and a decisive American victory that cost the Japanese two battleships (*Yamishiro* and *Fuso*).

Louisville came through the furious fighting around Leyte Gulf without major wounds and had been fortunate enough not to receive damage during the Rennell Island fray, but the law of averages caught up with the cruiser in 1945. While still off the Philippines, the cruiser was struck on 6 January 1945 by two kamikazes. On 5 June 1945 off Okinawa she was hit again by a single kamikaze. Casualties were 32 killed and 56 wounded in January and one killed and 59 wounded in June.

At the end of hostilities *Louisville* evacuated POWs from China and accepted the surrender of several Japanese ships before returning to the United States. Decommissioned on 17 June 1946, the cruiser remained in reserve until sold for scrap 14 September 1959.

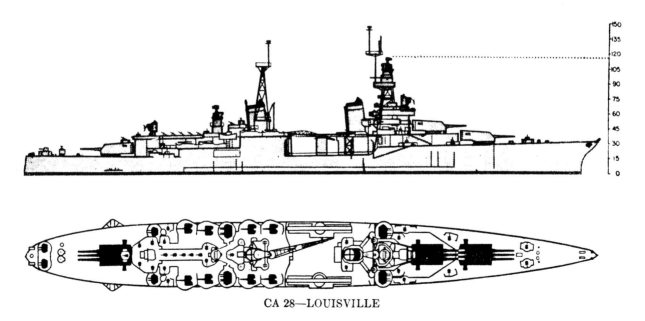

CA 28—LOUISVILLE

Hit by three kamikazes in the last eight months of the war, *Louisville* is seen here about to be hit in January 1945 while off the Philippines. This crash and another the same day took 32 lives. NA

CHICAGO CA-29

(3 Battle Stars) Honoring the city in Illinois, *Chicago* CA-29 was laid down 10 September 1928 at the Mare Island Navy Yard in Vallejo, Calif. She was sponsored at her launch 10 April 1930 by Miss Elizabeth Britten and was commissioned 9 March 1931. Her first commanding officer was Capt. M. Simons.

Like most of the major units of the U.S. Navy, *Chicago*'s home port for most of the 1930s was San Pedro, Calif. The ship transferred to Pearl Harbor in September 1940 and was at sea with the carrier *Lexington* (CV-2) en route to Midway to deliver planes when the Pacific war began. Her first experience in a combat area came in March and April 1942 while covering air attacks on Lae and Salamaua in New Guinea. In May the cruiser screened carrier *Yorktown* for the Tulagi raid and was part of the support group ordered to intercept the Japanese Port Moresby invasion force 7-8 May. As a result of the Battle of the Coral Sea, the enemy invasion force reversed course and never arrived to attack Port Moresby. However, *Chicago* and other units of the support group—detached from the carriers *Yorktown* and *Lexington* during the Battle of the Coral Sea—came under air attack. The cruiser suffered light casualties from strafing.

Chicago remained in the southwest Pacific for the summer of 1942 and was in support of the 7 August landings on Guadalcanal. During the night of 9 August *Chicago* was involved in the infamous Battle of Savo Island (see *Astoria* CA-34 for details of the battle). During this most disastrous surface battle for the U.S. Navy in the war, three American heavy cruisers were sunk, one Australian cruiser was lost, two American destroyers were fatally damaged and *Chicago* took one torpedo that killed two, wounded 21 and tore a gaping hole in the bow of the ship. Although blame for the disaster belonged on the shoulders of many, the captain of *Chicago* came in for special criticism for not alerting the other cruisers to the enemy's presence. Returning to San Francisco for repairs via Noumea and Sydney, Australia, *Chicago* did not return to the war zone until January 1943.

From August 1942 through January 1943 there were seven major naval battles in the contest for Guadalcanal. Three of the battles were surface battles (Savo Island, Cape Esperance and Tassafaronga), three were air-sea battles (Eastern Solomons, Santa Cruz and Rennell Island) and

Chicago under construction at Mare Island Navy Yard 9 April 1930. She was launched the following day.   USN

one—the 12-15 November Naval Battle of Guadalcanal—was fought on, above, and under the water. *Chicago* had the distinction of fighting in the first of these seven battles (Savo Island) and the last (Rennell Island).

The Rennell Island fight would perhaps more properly be termed the Battle "off" Rennell Island because that island itself was not the objective of the battle. At issue was Guadalcanal. Since American intelligence thought the Japanese were about to attempt yet another effort to reinforce the island (the enemy buildup of ships would actually be used for the evacuation of remaining troops), a large contingent of American troops was ordered to Guadalcanal. *Chicago* sailed forth to help protect the convoy.

In the twilight of 29 January, 31 enemy torpedo-bombers attacked TF 18 which was comprised of heavy cruisers *Chicago, Louisville* and *Wichita*, light cruisers *Cleveland* CL-55, *Montpelier* CL-57 and *Columbia* CL-56, and six destroyers (two escort carriers and two destroyers of TF 18 were lagging some miles away due to the slow speed of the CVEs). Despite some good shooting, *Chicago* took two aerial torpedoes on her starboard side soon after dark as the enemy used flares and the flames of burning planes to illuminate the American ships. Dead in the water by 2000 hours, *Chicago* was in serious trouble. After four hours of difficult work a tow line was passed from sister ship *Louisville* and the wounded cruiser began moving away from danger at four knots. After sunrise the tug *Navajo* relieved *Louisville* and the tow continued but at 1600 hours on 30 January, some three hours after the other cruisers had moved away, *Chicago* was again under air attack. Despite help from fighters flying from *Enterprise*, which was approximately 70 miles distant, the cruiser took four additional torpedo hits on the already damaged starboard side. Only 20 minutes later *Chicago* slid under the waves stern first with aproximately 10 percent of her complement still within.

Chicago sinking off Rennell Island 30 January 1943 after taking six aerial torpedoes.   USN

HOUSTON CA-30

(2 Battle Stars, Presidential Unit Citation) One of only three American cruisers to win the Presidential Unit Citation, *Houston* (CA-30) lived only a few weeks into World War II, but her short life was long on quality and courage. Her name would be passed to another famous cruiser (CL-81), but, unlike ill-fated sister ships *Northampton* and *Chicago*, her surviving crew members would not be reassigned to other warships. Their fight was for life itself inside Japanese prison camps.

Named for the city in Texas which she visited twice, *Houston* (CA-30) was laid down 1 May 1928 at Newport News Shipbuilding and Dry Dock Co. in Virginia. She was sponsored at her launch 7 September 1929 by Miss Elizabeth Holcombe and was commissioned 17 June 1930. Her first captain was J.B. Gray.

Early in 1931 *Houston* became the flagship of the Asiatic Station and was quite active in protecting American interests throughout the region after fighting erupted between Japan and China. Relieved by sister ship *Augusta* (CA-31) on 17 November 1933, *Houston* returned to the West Coast. During the summer of 1934 *Houston* was host to President Roosevelt for a long cruise and again em-

Houston in the Houston ship channel soon after being commissioned in 1930.   USN

Houston leads battleships *California* and *West Virginia* off Puerto Rico during one of President Roosevelt's cruises, 28 February 1939.

USN

barked the President for another cruise in 1935. For a short period in late 1938 the cruiser served as flagship of the U.S. Fleet. She spent late 1939 and early 1940 in Hawaiian waters and became flagship of the Asiatic Fleet 19 November 1940.

In the first weeks of war *Houston* was joined with warships of Australia, Britain, and the Netherlands (ABDA) in an attempt to hold the Indonesian area. Very early, control of the air went to the Japanese and during one raid on 4 February 1942 *Houston* took a bomb hit that killed over 50 men and burned out the aft 8-inch gun turret. On 15 February the cruiser again came under heavy air attack while covering a convoy, but once more managed to discourage enemy planes with withering anti-aircraft fire.

On 26 February *Houston* teamed with the British heavy cruiser *Exeter*, the Australian light cruiser *Perth*, Dutch light cruisers *DeRuyter* and *Java* and 10 Allied destroyers to oppose any enemy naval force moving to invade Java. In the late afternoon of the 26th, four Japanese cruisers (*Nachi, Haguro, Naka* and *Jintsu*) and 13 destroyers intervened between their transports and the ABDA force and for seven hours the Battle of the Java Sea raged. Although a fairly even match on paper, the ABDA force was greatly hindered by lack of training as a unit, by severe communication problems including a language gap between Dutch-and English-speaking commands, and by the lack of spotter planes, which had been detached from the ABDA force. The Japanese, on the other hand, did not suffer from these problems and they made especially good use of their spotter planes to direct gunfire. *Houston* could

fight only with her two forward 8-inch turrets, and without aerial spotters she could not see through smoke screens emitted by enemy destroyers. Later, sight was hindered by darkness. Japanese planes dropped flares after nightfall and by midnight the Japanese had received only minute damage while the Allied force had lost *Exeter, Java, DeRuyter*, three destroyers and the force commander, Rear Adm. K.W.F.M. Doorman. Just before his flagship (*Java*) went down, Admiral Doorman ordered *Houston* and *Perth* to retire.

The following day it was obvious that the defense of Java was a lost cause for the Allies. On the evening of the 27th, *Houston* and *Perth* were attempting to escape to Australia via Sunda Strait. Entering Banten Bay, the two cruisers discovered enemy transports—their main objective in the previous day's battle—and opened fire. Before leaving Banten Bay, and four severely damaged transports, the two Allied warships were surrounded by three enemy cruisers (*Mogami, Mikuma* and *Natori*) and a dozen destroyers. A wild battle ensued that could go only one way. Shortly after midnight *Perth* went down and then all enemy guns and torpedoes were directed at *Houston*. Before 0100 on 1 March 1942 the heroic cruiser succumbed to the overwhelming firepower of the enemy. Over 700 officers and men died and fewer than 300 survived enemy prison camps. When the full story of *Houston* became known after the war, Capt. A.H. Rooks was awarded the Medal of Honor (posthumously) and *Houston* was awarded the Presidential Unit Citation.

This painting by Joe T. Fleischman depicts the final moments of *Houston* March 1942.   USN

-23-

AUGUSTA CA-31

(3 Battle Stars) Few ships can claim to have touched as much of American history as did *Augusta*. Her receipt of only three battle stars and her absence from the Pacific during the war is deceptive when we understand the eventful life of this cruiser.

Named for the city in Georgia, *Augusta* (CA-31) was laid down 2 July 1928 by the Newport News Shipbuilding and Dry Dock Co., Newport News, Va. She was sponsored at her launch 1 February 1930 by Miss Evelyn McDaniel and was commissioned 30 January 1931. *Augusta's* first captain was J.O. Richardson, who would later rise to command the Pacific Fleet.

In July 1937 *Augusta* was the first American warship to visit Vladivostok, U.S.S.R. Assigned to the Asiatic Fleet since 1933, the cruiser answered the call of trouble in August 1937 when the Sino-Japanese War renewed with vigor. On "Bloody Saturday," 14 August 1937, the ship arrived in Shanghai and was promptly bombed by "friendly" Chinese planes. The bombs barely missed. Less than a week later, on 20 August, a shell believed fired from a Japanese gun killed one sailor and wounded several *Augusta* crewmen. And in December 1937 *Augusta* received on board survivors of the sunken American gunboat *Panay*.

The *Northampton*-class cruisers were intended to serve as flagships—additional accommodations were built into *Chicago*, *Houston* and *Augusta*—and *Augusta* had a notable history in this role. Leaving her role as flagship of the Asiatic Fleet in 1940, *Augusta* moved to the Atlantic in April 1941 to assume the same role there. In August *Augusta* carried President Roosevelt (who at one time or another visited or traveled on nearly every prewar heavy cruiser) to meet Prime Minister Winston Churchill at Placentia Bay, Newfoundland, for the famous "Atlantic Charter" conference. There, the leaders of the United States and Britain agreed to state the reasons why they would enter war with Japan (if Japan attacked British or Dutch possessions), agreed to supply the U.S.S.R., which had been invaded by Germany two months earlier, and agreed on a statement of principles concerning freedom.

Augusta's prewar experience in the Pacific was eventful. The cruiser's nearness to the fighting between the Japanese and the Chinese resulted in the loss of one *Augusta* crewmember not long after this picture was taken in Shanghai, August 1937.

USN

-24-

Augusta and HMS *Prince of Wales*, which had only two months to live, bring President Roosevelt and Prime Minister Churchill together 10-12 August 1941 in Placentia Bay, Newfoundland, for the Atlantic Charter Conference.

During World War II *Augusta* was present for the invasion of North Africa in November 1942 and participated in the action near Casablanca to repel Vichy French warships. In 1943 she escorted the *Queen Mary*, carrying Churchill to New York, served on the Murmansk convoy route, and was overhauled in November. Back on duty in the late spring of 1944, she bombarded the Normandy coast during the D-Day invason and delivered Gen. Omar Bradley to the battle site. From 15 August through 25 September 1944 the cruiser supported the invasion of southern France.

On 7 July 1945 President Harry Truman traveled to Antwerp, Belgium, for the Potsdam Conference on board *Augusta*. After the meeting, at which the call was made for Japan to surrender unconditionally, the cruiser returned the new president to Newport News. Immediately after the war *Augusta* joined the "Magic Carpet" fleet to bring home American troops from Europe.

This cruiser had seen war in the Pacific four years before it was declared but never fought in that ocean after the declaration. She was placed out of commission on 16 July 1946. Sold for scrap in 1959, *Augusta* died on the Hackensack River at Kearny, N.J., in the exact location where a host of other great ships of the era would die.

On the Hackensack River at Kearny, N.J., in 1960, *Augusta* awaits the scrapper's torch. *Enterprise* (CV-6), *Antietam* (CV-36), *Essex* (CV-9), *Franklin D. Roosevelt* (CV-42) and other famous ships of the era died at this same location. Hoffmann Collection

THE PORTLAND CLASS

DURING WORLD WAR II THE TWO MEMBERS OF THE *Portland* class, *Portland* (CA-33) and *Indianapolis* (CA-35), recorded outstanding combat service records. *Portland* earned 16 battle stars and *Indianapolis*, the last major American warship to be lost, garnered 10.

Even though they were authorized by the same February 1929 legislation that produced the later *San Francisco* class, the appearance of the *Portlands* was markedly similar to the overall design of the earlier *Northampton* class. Built at a cost of approximately $11 million each, these treaty cruisers carried a complement of about 700 officers and men before the war and about 1,200 in combat. The two *Portlands* were 10 feet longer than the *Northamptons* and 25 feet longer than the *Pensacolas* at 610' 3" overall but were similar to the two earlier classes in beam (66' 1"). In displacement the *Portlands* were heavier (9,950 tons for *Portland*; 9,800 for *Indianapolis*) and had a deeper average draft at 17'6". Like the earlier classes, top speed was just over 32 knots and horsepower was 107,000. Both ships had four shafts and possessed a cruising range of 9,800 miles at 15 knots or 4,700 miles at 25 knots.

Protection for *Portland* and *Indianapolis* was better than for either the *Pensacolas* or *Northamptons* in both thickness and distribution. The two cruisers had 3- to 4-inch side armor and 2-inch plus 2-inch deck armor. Turret sides were 1.5-inch, turret tops were 3 inches and turret faces were 5 inches thick.

The *Portlands* carried four float planes that could be launched from either of two catapults located amidships, again similar to earlier classes. Too, armament would be the same as that of the *Northamptons*: nine 8-inch guns in three turrets, two fore and one aft. Eventually the *Portlands* would carry eight 5-inch guns, but initially they carried only four. Throughout the ships' operational lives, anti-aircraft weaponry would be improved in both quality and quantity. Toward the end of their wartime careers the cruisers carried twenty-four 40mm intermediate-range guns and thirty-two 20 mm Oerlikon guns.

PORTLAND CA-33

(**16 Battle Stars, Navy Unit Commendation**) One of the four most combat-active cruisers of World War II, *Portland* (CA-33) was laid down 17 February 1929 by Bethlehem Shipbuilding in Quincy, Mass. She was sponsored at her launch on 21 May 1932 by Mrs. R.D. Brooks of Portland, Me., and was commissioned 23 February 1933. Her first commander was Capt. H.F. Leary.

In less than six weeks from the time of her commissioning, *Portland* rendered direct service when she was the first Navy ship to arrive at the crash site of the dirigible *Akron*. The disaster, which claimed 73 lives, took the life of Adm. William Moffett, chief of the Bureau of Aeronautics. Rescue operations off the coast of New England were conducted by *Portland*, but only three survivors were picked up.

Training and goodwill cruises occupied most of *Portland*'s time prior to war. When war arrived *Portland* was with *Lexington* (CV-2) headed for Midway, and her duties from 7 December 1941 until May 1942 centered on convoy duty primarily between Hawaii and the West Coast.

The first of many combat actions for *Portland* came during the Battle of the Coral Sea where she screened *Lexington*. On 8 May she took aboard 722 *Lexington* crewmen after the carrier went down. Only four weeks later she was in the screen for *Yorktown* at the Battle of Midway and once again saw an American carrier mortally wounded.

On 7 August 1942 *Portland* helped cover the invasion of Guadalcanal. The cruiser missed the Savo Island debacle as she was an escort for *Enterprise*, but this duty put her squarely in the middle of the furious air-sea Battle of the Eastern Solomons on 24 August. Again in support of *Enterprise*, *Portland* fought in the 26 October 1942 air-sea Battle of Santa Cruz. Constantly stymied in efforts to adequately suport their garrison on Guadalcanal and prevent American reinforcements, the Japanese tried again on 12-15 November 1942. In this momentous Naval Battle of Guadalcanal (see *San Francisco* for details) *Portland* fought in the 13 November action in which the United States lost two cruisers (*Atlanta* and *Juneau*) and four destroyers while the Japanese lost one battleship (*Hiei*) and two destroyers. *Portland* was hit by a torpedo on the starboard quarter that tore away both inboard props, jammed the aft 8-inch turret and distorted the stern so that she could steam only in circles. Continuing the fight despite her damage, *Portland* scored major hits on the enemy battlewagon *Hiei* which contributed to the eventual sinking of that ship. She also poured 8-inch shells into the already damaged enemy destroyer *Yudachi*, which blew up and sank. The sight of the sinking enemy warship was among the proudest moments for the crew of *Portland*.

Damage incurred during the November 1942 battle required major attention and *Portland* was lost to the fleet for the early months of 1943. Repaired, the cruiser was ordered to the Aleutians and on 26 July 1943 she bombarded Kiska. From November 1943 through February 1944 the cruiser served in the Gilberts and Marshalls and then operated in carrier screens as the Navy's move across the Pacific gained momentum. In September *Portland* bombarded Peleliu and in October she was with the fleet for the invasion of the Philippines. On 24 October *Portland* contributed to the sinking of two enemy battleships and three destroyers during the night action at Surigao Strait.

In February 1945 *Portland* bombarded Corregidor and in the spring the cruiser covered the Okinawa invasions. Constantly under attack from the air, *Portland* maintained station and provided continuing anti-aircraft fire and bombardment support. In September the cruiser was the site of the official surrender of the Caroline Islands. Postwar duties included the enjoyable task of returning servicemen to the continental United States, and in late October she steamed to Portland, Me., to help celebrate the nation's most festive Navy Day. Decommissioned 12 July 1946 the cruiser was maintained in reserve until sold for scrap 6 October 1959.

Portland laying smoke off Leyte in October 1944.   USN

INDIANAPOLIS CA-35

(10 Battle Stars) It would not be fair or proper to pass judgment on which ship loss was the most tragic during World War II, but if it were, *Indianapolis* (CA-35) would have a claim to the dubious distinction. Named for the capital of Indiana, *Indianapolis* was laid down 31 March 1930 by the New York Shipbuilding Corp. in Camden, N.J. She was sponsored at her launching ceremony on 7 November 1931 by Miss Lucy Taggart and was commissioned 15 November 1932. Her first commander was Capt. John M. Smeallie.

Indianapolis, like other prewar heavy cruisers, spent most of her time in training and tactical war problems from 1932 until 7 December 1941. Too, as flagship she hosted numerous dignitaries including President Roosevelt and Secretary of the Navy Claude A. Swanson.

The first year of war for *Indianapolis* was unlike the first year for other heavy cruisers; *Indianapolis* did not participate in the Solomons Campaign. After supporting carrier raids against Lae and Salamaua in New Guinea in March 1942, *Indianapolis* was overhauled at San Francisco. When again ready for duty the cruiser escorted a convoy to Australia and was then ordered to the Aleutians. In August 1942 *Indianapolis* bombarded Kiska, in January 1943 she supported the occupation of Amchitka and on 19 February she destroyed an enemy cargo ship which exploded with such violence that it is believed to have been carrying ammunition. With Attu retaken in May and Kiska evacuated by the enemy in August 1943, *Indianapolis* was ordered to San Francisco for refit. From November 1943 into February 1944 the cruiser partici-

Indianapolis passing under the Golden Gate Bridge, San Francisco, 1938. USN

As the fleet passes in review, President Roosevelt watches from *Indianapolis*, 31 May 1934. USN

pated in the Gilberts-Marshalls campaigns, moved into the Western Carolines in March and April 1944, and then supported the invasion of the Marianas in June. After another assignment to the Western Carolines in September, *Indianapolis* returned to San Francisco for overhaul.

Returning to the war in February 1945, *Indianapolis* screened carriers whose planes attacked the Japanese home islands, supported the Iwo Jima invasion and then moved on to participate in the pre-invasion bombardment of Okinawa. The day before the invasion of Okinawa, 31 March 1945, a kamikaze dove on *Indianapolis* and began the chain of events that led to the loss of the ship. For taking a direct hit, *Indianapolis* initially fared well. The plane itself did little damage and the bomb killed only nine men. But the bomb passed through the ship before exploding beneath and it was necessary for the cruiser to return to San Francisco for repairs. Repaired, *Indianapolis* was "available" in July 1945 and because she was a big, fast ship she was ordered on a mission to carry the uranium core of the Hiroshima atom bomb to Tinian. The crew was not aware of the details of the secret mission but responded to the order by setting a speed record from the West Coast to Tinian.

Indianapolis had made the rapid run from San Francisco to Tinian unescorted, but when assigned to the Philippines-Okinawa area via Guam after completing the secret mission the cruiser requested an escort. Despite being available no destroyer was assigned. Departing Tinian alone, passengers were deposited on Guam and the cruiser headed for Leyte. She would never arrive.

On the night of 29-30 July 1945 *Indianapolis* was struck on her starboard side by two torpedoes. Within 12 minutes the cruiser capsized and sank. Damage was so severe and time so short before sinking that the cruiser was unable to send a distress signal. It is believed that approximately 800 of 1,196 men were able to get off the cruiser before she went down. But, only 316 of this number would survive from those first minutes of Monday 30 July until Thursday noon 2 August. Without an escort destroyer, without capacity to send an SOS, and without a regulation requiring the Navy to search for overdue combat vessels, survivors of the torpedo attack were left to their own meager resources. The few rafts, floating debris and life jackets that would lose buoyancy after a protracted period in the water were the only threads of hope for the men who faced an unknown destiny. For 107 hours survivors battled the heat of the sun, lack of fresh water, the salt water, and sharks. Discovered by a plane that was *not* searching for them, the fortunate 316 were finally rescued.

Capt. Charles B. McVay was the only captain of the 10 cruisers lost during World War II to be court-martialed. He was vindicated at length, however, and the ultimate blame for the *Indianapolis* disaster was placed at the feet of the Navy's regulations that allowed the missing ship to go unnoticed by proper authorities. Like the price of many other lessons learned during the war, the price was quite high for not requiring closer attention to overdue warships.

Indianapolis **enters New York Harbor 31 May 1934 to return President Roosevelt to land after reviewing the fleet.**
USN

Indianapolis under fire from Japanese shore batteries off Saipan in June 1944.　　USN

THE NEW ORLEANS CLASS

THE SEVEN MEMBERS OF THE *NEW ORLEANS* class—*New Orleans* (CA-32), *Astoria* (CA-34), *Minneapolis* (CA-36), *Tuscaloosa* (CA-37), *San Francisco* (CA-38), *Quincy* (CA-39) and *Vincennes* (CA-44)—were authorized in 1929. Originally this legislation authorized construction of 15 cruisers but the number was reduced to 10 to honor the 1931 London Conference agreements.

The history of this class is similar to that of the other treaty heavy cruisers in that each ship saw combat, made notable contributions and endured great pain. Like the *Northampton* class, the *New Orleans* class would lose three of its members. All three—*Astoria*, *Quincy* and *Vincennes*—were lost during the August 1942 Battle of Savo Island. But most significantly, the *New Orleans* class would claim the honor of having three of its ships in the top four in terms of the number of battle stars earned by cruisers, with *San Francisco* and *Minneapolis* topping the list. Too, *San Francisco* would garner one of the three Presidential Unit Citations awarded to cruisers for World War II service. Together the *New Orleans* class earned 63 battle stars (*New Orleans* 16, *Astoria* 3, *Minneapolis* 17, *Tuscaloosa* 7, *San Francisco* 17, *Quincy* 1 and *Vincennes* 2).

The *New Orleans*-class cruisers cost between $11 million and $15 million each. The difference in cost was due in part to the variance in profits of private shipbuilding yards over Navy yards and to the fact that these ships were built over a period of nearly seven years— September 1930 to February 1937. The complement of the *New Orleans* class did not vary noticeably from other heavy cruisers—approximately 700 officers and men in peacetime to nearly 1,200 in wartime. This class was, however, slightly different than the two preceding classes in length and beam as the *New Orleans* cruisers were shorter (588 feet overall) and had a thinner beam (61' 9"). Displacement, however, was as much or more than any other treaty cruiser at 9,950 tons (*Quincy* 9,375 and *Vincennes* 9,400). The weight saved in length and beam was added to protection and therefore the *New Orleans* cruisers had a deeper mean draft (19' 6"). Like earlier classes top speed was a little over 32 knots, horsepower was 107,000 and each ship had four shafts. Unlike earlier classes, the *New Orleans* cruisers had a shorter range (7,600 miles at 15 knots or 3,500 miles at 25 knots) due in part to a smaller fuel capacity of 2,256 tons.

Protection for the *New Orleans* cruisers was better than any of the earlier classes. All seven ships had 1.5-inch to 5-inch armor (thickest armor amidships),

3-inch plus 2-inch decks and 5-to 6-inch turret faces. Distribution of armor was continuous from below turret number one to turret number three; some 400 feet were thus covered just above and below the waterline.

The *New Orleans* class normally carried four float planes to be launched from two catapults. The hangars and catapults were located farther aft in this class than earlier classes. In later cruiser classes that carried planes except the Alaskas (anti-aircraft cruisers of the *Atlanta-Oakland* class did not carry planes) hangar space and catapult(s) would be moved to the stern.

Armament for this class followed the pattern of other heavy cruisers except the *Pensacolas*. Once again 8-inch guns would be placed in two triple turrets fore and one aft. Secondary armament, as usual, was eight 5-inch open mounts. Later in the war surviving members of the class would carry up to twenty-four 40mm and twenty-eight 20 mm.

As mentioned earlier, numerous modifications from commissioning dates to the end of the war changed the appearance of the treaty cruisers. Still, the *New Orleans* class differed from earlier cruisers in overall appearance from the beginning not only due to the more aft location of hangars and catapults but also because this class did not have a clipper bow or an overhang along the bows. Too, the bridges of the *New Orleans*-class cruisers were raised and the funnel arrangement was markedly different.

Less than a month after this picture was taken, three of the four cruisers closest to the camera would be lost in the August 1942 Battle of Savo Island. Those to die were *Astoria* (bottom), *Vincennes* (second from the bottom) and *Quincy* (third from bottom). Fourth from the bottom is the cruiser *New Orleans*. *NA*

(16 Battle Stars) Named for the "city of dreams and jazz," *New Orleans* (CA-32) was laid down 14 March 1931 by the New York Navy Yard. She was sponsored by Miss Cora S. Jahncke at the cruiser's launch on 12 April 1933 and was commissioned 15 February 1934. Capt. Allen B. Reed was the ship's first commander.

In her seven years before the war, *New Orleans* trained with the fleet. Having served out of Hawaii since 12 October 1939, the cruiser was in Pearl Harbor on the morning of the attack. Like most other ships in the harbor that fateful Sunday morning, *New Orleans* was not ready for combat. With her engines under repair and the ship dependent upon external sources for power, she could not escape the melee. Still, guns were fired manually and the cruiser began her combat career within minutes of the war's beginning. Fortunately, only one bomb exploded near the ship and injuries were relatively light.

New Orleans took time from her repairs to convoy troops to Johnston Island and then she reported to San Francisco on 13 January 1942 to complete repairs. Ready a month later, the cruiser escorted a convoy to Australia. In April *New Orleans* joined with a task force built around *Yorktown* and helped screen the carrier during the May 1942 Battle of the Coral Sea. Boat crews from *New Orleans* assisted in the rescue of several hundred men from the sinking *Lexington* before the cruiser left the area with the wounded *Yorktown*. Less than a month later *New Orleans* screened *Enterprise* at the Battle of Midway.

In August 1942 *New Orleans* was part of the screen for carrier *Saratoga*, and when *Sara* was torpedoed 31 August the cruiser escorted her to Pearl. Upon arrival back in the Solomons in late November, the cruiser was included in a hastily assembled group of four heavy cruisers, one light cruiser and six destroyers. This force dueled a Japanese destroyer force on the night of 30 November-1 December 1942 (see *Northampton* for details of the Battle of Tassafaronga). Sheering away from the wounded flagship *Minneapolis*, *New Orleans* steamed into the path of an enemy torpedo. The tremendous explosion tore off 120 feet of the forward section of the ship including the number one 8-inch turret. There were no survivors from the lost bow. As the severed bow slid down the port side of the cruiser it gouged holes in the hull. On the aft portion of the cruiser, some crewmen thought they had run over a sinking *Minneapolis*.

On fire, taking water, and with continued power unsure, *New Orleans* was a candidate for the bottom. But, improved damage control since the Savo Island disaster and the resourcefulness of the crew kept the ship from sinking. After a slow, tenuous, short journey to Tulagi, initial repairs—including a jury-rigged coconut log bow—were made. From Tulagi the cruiser steamed to Australia for repairs and from there she traveled to Bremerton, Wash. for the installation of a new bow.

New Orleans rejoined the war in October 1943, participating in a raid on Wake Island (5-6 October), the taking of the Gilberts and Marshalls (November 1943-February 1944), the raid on Truk (17-18 February 1944), and supported the landings at Hollandia, New Guinea. Although

New Orleans off the coast of England in June 1934. Note the paucity of anti-aircraft guns and lack of splinter shields for 5-inch guns.
USN

not a prime target as a screen ship for a carrier, a cruiser was nonetheless in danger from enemy action and, on occasion, from friends. On 22 April 1944 one crewmember was killed and others wounded when an American carrier plane hit *New Orleans'* mainmast, sprayed the cruiser with fuel, and exploded alongside.

In June 1944 *New Orleans* bombarded the Marianas, screened carriers during the Battle of the Philippine Sea in the same month, and supported the return to the Philippines in October. Leaving for overhaul in December 1944, the cruiser returned to the war, now off Okinawa, in April 1945. Here she fired her last rounds in anger. Returning from the war *New Orleans* spent 10 days in her namesake city in early 1946 before moving on to Philadelphia 12 March 1946. Decommissioned 10 February 1947 the cruiser remained in reserve until sold for scrap 22 September 1959.

The severely damaged *New Orleans* camouflaged in Tulagi Harbor after the 30 November-1 December 1942 Battle of Tassafaronga. NA

New Orleans with temporary bow in December 1942. Compare this picture with the photo taken in 1934 to appreciate the magnitude of damage. NA

Cover of the memorial issue of the Japan Times Weekly, published in Tokyo 20 April 1939 on the occasion of the arrival of Ambassador Saito's ashes aboard *Astoria*. Ironically, *Astoria* would be sunk some three years later by the Japanese in the Battle of Savo Island. USN

THE JAPAN TIMES WEEKLY
A Comprehensive Survey of Current Events and National Activities

VOL. II, NO. 16   TOKYO, THURSDAY, APRIL 20, 1939   PRICE: 40 SEN

SPECIAL FEATURES: Messages from HACHIRO ARITA, Japanese Foreign Minister, Admiral MITSUMASA YONAI, Japanese Navy Minister and JOSEPH CLARK GREW, American Ambassador to Tokyo

THE SAITO I KNEW   IN MEMORIAM

Sailors from *Astoria* carry the ashes of Hiroshi Saito, Japanese ambassador to the United States, to Japanese officials at Yokohama 17 April 1939. *Astoria* is in the background. USN

(3 Battle Stars) One of the three ill-fated cruisers of the *New Orleans* class to be sunk at the Battle of Savo Island, *Astoria* (CA-34) was laid down 1 September 1930 by the Puget Sound Navy Yard, Bremerton, Wash. She was sponsored at her launch on 16 December 1933 by Mrs. Leila C. McKey and was commissioned 28 April 1934. *Astoria*'s first captain was E.S. Root.

The highlight and most ironic event of *Astoria*'s prewar service occurred in the spring of 1939 when the ship was chosen to carry the ashes of Hiroshi Saito, former Japanese ambassador to Washington, to Yokohama. *Astoria*'s commander at the time of this mission was Capt. Richmond Kelly Turner who during the upcoming war would rise to flag rank and be a major thorn to the Japanese. But in April 1939 *Astoria* and Captain Turner were properly received and the goodwill mission temporarily interrupted deteriorating diplomatic relations between the future antagonists.

On 7 December 1941 *Astoria* was with the *Lexington* en route to Midway. From February 1942 *Astoria* operated in the screen for *Yorktown* and was with that carrier during early raids into the Marshalls and Gilberts. In May and June 1942 the cruiser screened *Yorktown* during the Battles of the Coral Sea and Midway. On 7 August 1942 she covered the Marine landings on Guadalcanal and on Saturday evening 8 August she took up patrol in the waters north of Guadalcanal, soon to be named "Ironbottom Sound."

The Battle of Savo Island took place in these waters just after midnight in the early minutes of Sunday 9 August 1942. It was one of the worst disasters ever to occur in American military history. Courage was not missing during that night, but intelligence (of all kinds) and alertness were deficient. The seven enemy cruisers (heavy cruisers *Chokai, Aoba, Kako, Kinugasa* and *Furutaka*; light cruisers *Tenryu* and *Yubari*) and destroyer *Yunagi* under the command of Vice Adm. Gunichi Mikawa had been sighted heading for the landing area on Guadalcanal and Tulagi. However, the sightings reported some of the cruisers as being seaplane tenders and destroyers and this led American commanders to discount a night surface action and anticipate an air raid after daybreak. Too, associated messages were delayed and the decision of Adm. F.J. Fletcher to remove his carriers from the area added diversions to the thoughts of the American command. Just before the battle began Rear Adm. R.K. Turner called a meeting that removed Rear Adm. V. A. C. Crutchley of the Royal Navy from his cruiser command; the already divided Allied command was further weakened.

Considering the fact that a night surface action was not expected, the Allied ships were properly disposed. The Northern Force, which included *Astoria, Quincy* and *Vincennes*, guarded the approach to the Sound north of Savo; the Southern Force, including *Chicago* (CA-29) and Australian heavy cruiser *Canberra* (heavy cruiser *Australia* was temporarily away transporting Crutchley to his meeting with Admiral Turner and Gen. A.A. Vandegrift), guarded the approach south of Savo; and light cruiser *San Juan* (CL-54) with an Australian cruiser and two American destroyers watched the eastern and most unlikely approach for enemy warships. Aboard the Allied cruisers only half the crews were on watch and captains were away from their respective bridges. Convectional showers obscured vision and the several planes above the formations were believed to be Allied planes, or, if enemy planes, they were only scouts for the enemy that was expected after daybreak.

The Japanese stormed into the Sound south of Savo with numerous factors working to their advantage, including continued poor communications among the Allies even after the Japanese were known to be in the Sound. At 0143 the battle began. Taken by surprise, the Australian cruiser *Canberra* was struck by two torpedoes and gunfire and was out of the fight before she ever got into it. With 84 men dead she went down soon after daybreak. *Chicago* took a torpedo that tore off a small section of its bow and the American cruiser steamed off to the east away from the battle. Worse, *Chicago*'s captain, substituting for the missing Southern Force commander (Crutchley), did not notify the Northern Force of the situation. *Astoria*, last in line of the three Northern Force cruisers, was the first ship of that group to come under fire. As with both her sister ships she was seen first by the illumination of spotlights, but fires aboard, especially those caused by enemy shells in the spotter plane hangars, made her stand out distinctly to Japanese gun directors. Illuminated, unprepared, and outnumbered, the Allies' place in the battle's outcome was obvious. Despite getting in a few hits on the enemy flagship, *Astoria* was mauled. An effort was made to beach the ship but to no avail. At 1215 *Astoria*, the last of the four Allied cruisers to sink in the battle, went down with 216 of her dead still within.

Swinging 180 degrees around Savo Island, Admiral Mikawa led his ships away from the area. His great victory was somewhat muted in that he did not strike any blows to the transports. Too, he lost one cruiser (*Kako*) on the way northwest to an American submarine (*S-44*) on Monday the 10th. And finally, he demonstrated to the Allies numerous lessons on "how to" and "how not" to fight a night surface action.

(17 Battle Stars) *Minneapolis* (CA-36) tied sister ship *San Francisco* in battle stars earned for cruisers during World War II with 17. Due to an earlier tabulation error, the 17th battle star was not awarded until 1985. Named for the city in Minnesota, *Minneapolis* was laid down 27 June 1931 at the Philadelphia Navy Yard. She was sponsored at her launch 6 September 1933 by Miss Grace L. Newton and was commissioned 19 May 1934. Her first commander was Capt. Gordon W. Haines.

After her shakedown cruise to Europe, *Minneapolis* was destined to spend only a short period in the Atlantic before moving to the Pacific in the spring of 1935. Except for a cruise to the Caribbean in 1939 the cruiser operated in the Pacific during the prewar years.

Minneapolis and they began a search for the enemy. This force was reported by an *Enterprise* plane to be the enemy and the only American carrier in the area steamed south to join an uneven fight. Fortunately, this mismatch did not occur not only for *Enterprise* but also for the cruiser group operating without air cover.

Minneapolis was quite active in the early months of the war. In February and March she screened carriers during the raids into enemy territory and participated in the Battle of the Coral Sea and the Battle of Midway. In August the cruiser supported the invasion of Guadalcanal. On 30 August it was necessary for her to tow carrier *Saratoga* toward safety after *Saratoga* received her second disabling torpedo hit in less than eight months. Primarily serving as

Victim at Tassafaronga. *Minneapolis* sports a jury-rigged, coconut-log bow in early December 1942 as a result of a Japanese destroyer-launched torpedo.   NA

Minneapolis was one of the very few ships stationed at Pearl Harbor that was ready for a battle on the morning of 7 December 1941 as she was underway approximately 30 miles south of Oahu. Her routine that morning called for gunnery practice. In view of the fact that the Japanese had contingency plans for attacking American warships outside the harbor, it is somewhat surprising that *Minneapolis* and the four smaller ships with her were not attacked. By noon of that day several ships from Pearl, including light cruisers *Detroit, St. Louis* and *Phoenix,* joined

a screen for carriers in the early phases of the Solomons Campaign, *Minneapolis,* as flagship, was ordered to lead a cruiser-destroyer force to intercept an enemy surface force moving to bring supplies and fresh troops to Guadalcanal. Under the command of Rear Adm. C.H. Wright, the American force of four heavy cruisers, one light cruiser and six destroyers met the enemy squadron of eight destroyers on the night of 29-30 November (see *Northampton* for details of the Battle of Tassafaronga). During this action *Northampton* and one Japanese destroyer were sunk and the American heavy cruisers were severely damaged. The first of the three American cruisers to be hit was *Minneapolis*. After firing nine 8-inch salvos, which helped sink the enemy destroyer *Takanami*, *Minneapolis* took one torpedo on her port bow and another in her number two fireroom. Using the flashes of American guns as aiming points, the Japanese held their gunfire but scored mightily with their fast, powerful torpedoes.

Within moments the bow of the cruiser, all the way to the number one turret, dropped beneath the surface. Fire covered the ship forward of the bridge for a few moments but seawater thrown up by the underwater blasts smothered the flames. Although there was sufficient power to fire the forward 8-inch guns three more times, the cruiser was in great danger. Minutes later, power to fire the forward guns was gone, speed was down, and the ship was listing slightly and taking water rapidly. By masterful display of courage and application of damage control *Minneapolis* was able to move toward Tulagi at three knots. A few days after the battle at Tulagi the effort to save the cruiser by crew and Seabees nearly went for naught when a gas explosion nearly sank the ship. But by 12 December,

Minneapolis, minus her bow and a significant number of crewmen lost on 30 November, was on her way to San Francisco via Espiritu Santo and Pearl Harbor.

With a new bow and replacements for the men lost off Tassafaronga, *Minneapolis* returned to the Pacific war in August 1943. Except for the fight at Iwo Jima *Minneapolis* would participate in all the remaining major operations in that theater. Her guns would pound enemy positions and cover carriers in the Gilberts, Marshalls (late 1943, early 1944), Carolines, Marianas and Philippines (1944) and Okinawa (1945). The cruiser won particular praise for her gunfire support at Guam (August 1944), and she was present for the historic big-gun action at Surigao Strait during the October 1944 Battle of Leyte Gulf. Away from the war in its last weeks to replace the burned linings of her guns, the cruiser, flying the flag of Adm. Thomas Kincaid, served as the site for the acceptance of the surrender of Korea on 9 September 1945. Returning to the United States with additional passengers on board, the ship was decommissioned 10 February 1947 and sold for scrap 14 August 1959.

Minneapolis at Espiritu Santo in January 1943 with a temporary bow for the voyage back to the United States for permanent repairs.
USN

TUSCALOOSA CA-37

(**7 Battle Stars**) *Tuscaloosa* (CA-37) was one of the few combat ships of World War II to fight in both the Atlantic and Pacific and not receive major damage or suffer major casualties. This charmed cruiser, named for the city in Alabama, was laid down 3 September 1931 by the New York Shipbuilding Co. She was sponsored by Mrs. Thomas Lee McCann at the launching ceremony 15 November 1933 and was commissioned 17 August 1934.

From the spring of 1935 until the winter of 1939 *Tuscaloosa* was based in the Pacific. Already in the Atlantic when war began in Europe, she was immediately ready to participate in the Neutrality Patrol. On 19 December 1939 the German liner *Columbus* was scuttled when challenged by the British destroyer *Hyperion*. At the request of *Hyperion*'s captain, *Tuscaloosa* received aboard nearly 600 passengers and crew of the *Columbus* and carried them to New York. Other highlights of the cruiser's prewar career centered on the transport of President Roosevelt to Central America (February-March 1940) and to the Caribbean (December 1942) to inspect base sites obtained from Britain in the "destroyers for bases" agreement. On this cruise the president conceived the lend-lease program that greatly assisted Britain during the dark and lonely hours when she alone defended the ramparts of democracy. *Tuscaloosa* was operating in the North Atlantic when the United States entered the war in December 1941. Patrol duty was replaced by convoy duty and the ship prepared to meet submarines and surface units of the German navy. After overhaul in the late summer of 1942, *Tuscaloosa* supported "Operation Torch," the Allied thrust into North Africa. The cruiser added her firepower to that of other Allied ships and took several near misses from shore batteries and from the incomplete Vichy French battleship *Jean Bart*. In October 1943 *Tuscaloosa* covered carrier *Ranger* during the first American carrier strikes against European targets and on 6 June 1944 she was off the coast of Normandy providing gunfire support for the D-Day invasion of the continent. On 26 June the cruiser and other Allied ships dueled German shore batteries at Cherbourg. And before leaving for the Pacific, *Tuscaloosa* bombarded enemy targets along the Italian coast.

In January 1945 *Tuscaloosa* joined the Third Fleet in the Pacific. First action was off Iwo Jima in February and March. Later in March the cruiser was on hand for the Okinawa operation, remaining there until its conclusion. At the end of the war *Tuscaloosa* transported veterans to San Francisco before steaming on to Philadelphia for decommissioning 13 February 1946. On 25 June 1959 she was sold for scrap.

Tuscaloosa in the Caribbean in the spring of 1939.   USN

Tuscaloosa and *Chicago* undergoing refit at Mare Island Navy Yard in 1936. Note number on turret roofs.   USN

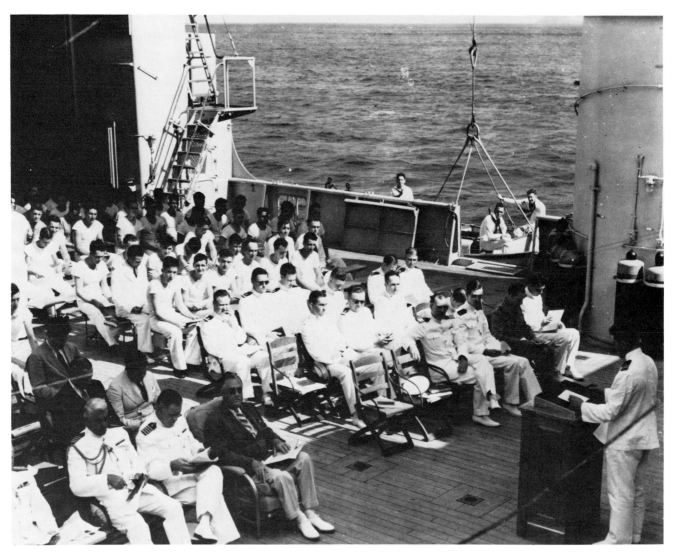

President Roosevelt aboard *Tuscaloosa* in 1940. The silver-haired officer to the President's right is Capt. Daniel Callaghan, then the President's naval aide and later an admiral who would lose his life aboard *San Francisco* in the heroic November 1942 Naval Battle of Guadalcanal.   USN

SAN FRANCISCO CA-38

(17 Battle Stars, Presidential Unit Citation) Of all the American ships to fight in World War II only the famed carrier *Enterprise* would receive more battle stars and honors than heavy cruiser *San Francisco* (CA-38). One of only three cruisers to win the Presidential Unit Citation, *San Francisco* earned 17 battle stars and, like *Enterprise*, she fought the enemy from Pearl Harbor in 1941 to the shores of Japan in 1945. Laid down 9 September 1931 by the Mare Island Navy Yard in the San Francisco metropolitan area, the cruiser was sponsored at her launch 9 March 1933 by Miss Barbara M. Bailly and was commissioned 10 February 1934. Her first captain was Royal E. Ingersoll.

One of the more unfortunate threads in American military history has been a lack of vigilance in defending installations potentially threatened by enemy action. The early Sunday morning terrorist attack against U.S. Marine and Navy personnel in Lebanon 23 October 1983 suggests the American military establishment has not yet learned this lesson. On Sunday morning 7 December 1941 *San Francisco* was as unprepared as a warship could have been. With her engineering plant apart for overhaul, ammunition in storage, new anti-aircraft mounts not yet installed and many officers and crewmen absent, the cruiser was in no condition to offer resistance to the Japanese. Fortunately *San Francisco* absorbed no damage in the attack and by the middle of December she was at sea having cut short some of the work planned for her overhaul.

For the early months of the war *San Francisco* operated

San Francisco returns to her namesake city for repairs after the Naval Battle of Guadalcanal.

with carrier *Lexington* during operations in the South Pacific. However, the cruiser was assigned convoy duty in late April 1942 from Pearl Harbor to the city for which she was named and then to New Zealand. Therefore she did not participate in either the Battle of the Coral Sea or the Battle of Midway. In August *San Francisco* arrived off the coast of Guadalcanal to cover the Marine invasion. The flagship for TF 18, *San Francisco* was with *Wasp* on 15 September when the carrier was lost. On the night of 11-12 October 1942 the cruiser was flagship of TF 64 when that force met two Japanese cruisers and six destroyers off Cape Esperance at the northwest corner of Guadalcanal (see *Salt Lake City* for details of the Battle of Cape Esperance.) The force, under the command of Rear Adm. Norman Scott aboard *San Francisco*, achieved the U.S. Navy's first night action victory over the Japanese by sinking heavy cruiser *Furutaka* and destroyer *Hatsuyuki* while losing destroyer *Duncan*. On 20 October the *San Francisco* barely missed disaster when she avoided submarine torpedoes, one of which did hit *Chester*.

From the beginning of the Guadalcanal Campaign in August 1942 until its end in February 1943 the strategic objective of each of the two antagonists was to occupy the island and evict the other. To do this it was necessary to land troops and supplies and prevent the other side from doing the same. All naval battles around Guadalcanal were fought to achieve this paramount objective and the 12-15 November battle was the decisive contest. In less than 72 hours the Japanese would lose 11 heavily loaded transports, two battleships (*Hiei* and *Kirishima*), heavy

cruiser *Kinugasa* and three destroyers (*Akatsuki*, *Yudachi* and *Ayanami*). The U.S. Navy would lose two anti-aircraft light cruisers (sister ships *Atlanta* and *Juneau*) and seven destroyers (*Barton*, *Monssen*, *Cushing*, *Laffey*, *Preston*, *Walke* and *Benham*).

The protracted three-day battle was touched off when both sides attempted major reinforcement efforts. During the second week of November 1942 seven American transport-cargo ships steamed from Noumea and Espiritu Santo, while from Truk came 11 enemy transports. On the afternoon of the 12th *San Francisco* was in the screen protecting the transports just off the coast of Guadalcanal when the American ships came under aerial torpedo attack. No transports were sunk and many enemy planes were shot down, but *San Francisco* was crashed into by a damaged enemy torpedo plane. The plane struck the aft control station. It destroyed the station as well as an anti-aircraft gun director and a fire control radar while 50 men were killed or wounded. Late that night the equipment and lost men would be sorely missed.

The arrival of Japanese battleships, cruisers and destroyers to bombard American positions around Henderson Field was expected. Even though all knew that the American force of two heavy cruisers, three light cruisers and eight destroyers was not an even match for the enemy, there would nonetheless be an attempt to stop the bombardment.

At 0145 on Friday the 13th of November, the 14 Japanese and 13 American warships met in Ironbottom Sound. After initial confusion, Rear Adm. Daniel J. Cal-

Fifty men were killed or wounded when a damaged enemy plane crashed into the aft superstructure (shown here) of *San Francisco* on the afternoon of 12 November. Later that night (the 13th) an additional 200 men were killed or wounded in the Naval Battle of Guadalcanal. USN

Close-up view of damage on the port side of *San Francisco*. Close examination with a magnifying glass indicates the cruiser was peppered by large-, medium- and small-caliber shells. USN

laghan, a former captain of *San Francisco*, gave the order to open fire. The 27 ships fought a fierce battle at close range for the better part of 30 minutes and then began to separate. Flagship of TF 67.4, *San Francisco* blazed away at several enemy ships including enemy battleship *Hiei*, but ceased fire when it appeared she was firing on *Atlanta*. Shortly thereafter *San Francisco* was hit by shells from the second enemy battleship, *Kirishima*, a cruiser and at least one destroyer. The bridge section and topsides of *San Francisco* were severely damaged by 45 hits and 81 officers and men, including Admiral Callaghan and Capt. Cassin Young, were lost. Despite tremendous topside damage the cruiser had not taken any shells or torpedoes below the waterline and she was able to leave the scene under her own power. By morning *San Francisco* was moving east leaving behind forever *Atlanta*, *Cushing*, *Laffey*, *Barton*, *Monssen* and two Japanese destroyers and battleship *Hiei*, which sank after further punishment from the air. Damaged *Juneau* was alongside *San Francisco* when a submarine torpedo destroyed the *Juneau* just before noon.

Of the 13 American ships that fought on the 13th, six were sunk and three, including cruisers *San Francisco* and *Portland*, were too badly damaged to fight again un-til repaired. Consequently, no effective American surface force was present to prevent bombardment on the night of 13-14 November, but on the night of 14-15 November American battleships *Washington* and *South Dakota* met the enemy and sank battleship *Kirishima* and destroyer *Ayanami*. Despite the defeat of their surface units, 11 loaded enemy transports headed for Guadalcanal only to have seven sunk and four beached by planes from Henderson Field and *Enterprise*.

For her significant contributions in this battle and the earlier Battle of Cape Esperance, *San Francisco* received the Presidential Unit Citation. Her damaged bridge was removed in January 1943 when the cruiser returned to Mare Island for repairs. The bridge still exists today as part of a memorial to the ship.

By late February 1943 *San Francisco* was back in the war. She steamed through the battles off Alaska, the Gilberts, Marshalls, Carolines, Marianas and Philippines. In December 1944 she rode out the infamous typhoon that caused the loss of three destroyers, and in 1945 she fought near the shores of Iwo Jima and Okinawa. Decommissioned 10 February 1946 the famous cruiser was sold for scrap 9 September 1959.

Repaired and ready to return to war, *San Francisco* is seen here in the winter of 1943. The white lines in-dicate areas of repair or additions. Note the more compact forward super-structure.   USN

QUINCY CA-39

(1 Battle Star) Lost with sister ships *Astoria* and *Vincennes* in the Battle of Savo Island, *Quincy* (CA-39) was laid down by the Bethlehem Shipbuilding Corp. on 15 November 1933 in the city for which she was named. *Quincy* was sponsored at her launching ceremony on 19 June 1935 by Mrs. Henry S. Morgan and was commissioned at Boston 9 June 1936. The cruiser's first commander was Capt. William F. Amsden.

Quincy was called upon for special assignment immediately after commissioning. Ordered to Spain to protect American interests threatened by the Spanish Civil War, *Quincy* joined an international rescue fleet which included the German pocket battleship *Admiral Graf Spee*. After removing several hundred people from the embattled country, *Quincy* returned to Boston to conclude her acceptance trials, which were completed in

March 1937. Operating in the Pacific for most of 1937 and 1938, the cruiser was deployed to the Atlantic in January 1939. From January 1939 until the summer of 1942 *Quincy* remained in the Atlantic for training. After the start of war in Europe, the cruiser steamed on Neutrality Patrol along the North Atlantic routes. Too, there were escort duties for convoys, some even as far south as South Africa.

After overhaul in the spring of 1942 *Quincy* was ordered to the Pacific. Her first assignment, the support of Marine landings on Guadalcanal, would be her last. After bombardment of enemy positions on 7 August the cruiser was assigned to cover the northern entrance into the Sound off Guadalcanal with sister ships *Astoria* and *Vincennes*. Unaware of the presence of enemy ships (see *Astoria* for details of the Battle of Savo Island), *Quincy*

Quincy at New York in 1939.

USN

was caught unprepared for action. Of the three American cruisers and one Australian heavy cruiser lost that early Sunday morning of 9 August 1942, *Quincy* absorbed the most damage and had the highest casualty list with 370 killed. Illuminated by enemy searchlights, *Quincy* managed to get off two 8-inch salvos but confusion on the bridge and fear of firing on Allied ships brought an order to cease fire. Soon thereafter *Quincy* was hit on the

bridge with great loss of life and consequent loss of direction for the battle. Enemy gunfire accuracy was aided by fires on the American vessel and a torpedo on the port side caused flooding that contributed to the cruiser's doom. At 0235 *Quincy* capsized to port and became the first of many American and Japanese warships to sink beneath the waves of "Ironbottom Bay."

Quincy illuminated by Japanese searchlights during the 9 August 1942 Battle of Savo Island. The picture was taken from a Japanese cruiser. Only minutes after this picture was taken *Quincy* capsized and sank—the first of many warships to rest on "Ironbottom Bay."   USN

VINCENNES CA-44

(2 Battle Stars)   *Vincennes* (CA-44), sunk with sister ships *Astoria* and *Quincy* at the Battle of Savo Island, was built alongside *Quincy* at the Bethlehem Shipbuilding Co.'s Fore River yard. Laid down 2 January 1934, the cruiser was sponsored by Miss Harriet V. Kimmell of Vincennes, Ind., at the launching on 21 May 1936. Commissioned 24 February 1937, the cruiser steamed to Europe on her shakedown cruise with Capt. Burton H. Green in command.

Vincennes visited the Pacific after commissioning but the bulk of her prewar time was spent in the Atlantic. Training, Neutrality Patrol, and convoy duty were her major assignments. After Pearl Harbor *Vincennes* reported to the East Coast and in March 1942 she entered the Pacific. Assigned to TF 18, *Vincennes*

escorted carrier *Hornet* (CV-8) to a rendezvous with TF 16 built around *Enterprise* and then steamed with the two forces to launch the 18 April 1942 Halsey-Doolittle raid on Japan. Too late to participate in the Battle of the Coral Sea three weeks later, *Vincennes* prepared to screen carriers in the June 1942 Battle of Midway. During the attack on *Yorktown*, *Vincennes* gunners accounted for at least one enemy plane.

After returning to Pearl *Vincennes* was ordered to cover the Marine landings on Guadalcanal and Tulagi. While covering these landings on 7 and 8 August, *Vincennes* claimed nine enemy planes. Unwanted excitement was also provided by having to dodge an enemy aerial torpedo.

As part of the Northern Force assigned to cover the

still unloading transports off Lunga Point, Guadalcanal, *Vincennes* joined sister ships *Astoria* and *Quincy* in a slow box movement around the northern approaches of the Sound (see *Astoria* for details of the Battle of Savo Island). She was the last of the three American cruisers to be engaged in the Savo Island fight, but *Vincennes* was nonetheless terribly hurt before she could adequately respond. Although she did get off a few rounds and did hit one ship, *Vincennes* was illuminated by fires onboard and Japanese shells quickly rendered the topsides helpless. Two or three torpedoes ended her fight against the enemy—and her fight for life. At 0250 *Vincennes* capsized with a loss of 332 men.

Vincennes passing through the Panama Canal 6 January 1938. USN

Vincennes steams past the moratally wounded *Yorktown* during the Battle of Midway 4 June 1942. NA

THE WICHITA CLASS

WICHITA CA-45

(**13 Battle Stars**) Authorized in 1929 and orginally intended to be a unit of the *New Orleans* class, *Wichita* (CA-45) became the 18th and last heavy cruiser to be built under the limitations of the Washington and London treaties. Active throughout the war, *Wichita* fought in the Atlantic, Mediterranean and Pacific and by the end of hostilities she had earned 13 battle stars.

The cruiser was built at a cost of approximately $19 million and she carried a complement of approximately 1,000 men. Because her commissioning date was within six and a half months of the start of war in Europe, CA-45 did not have the significant increase of complement experienced by most other prewar heavy cruisers.

Wichita's appearance was a radical departure from all previous heavy cruisers in that she had a flush-deck hull, high transom stern, built-in protected fantail hangar and catapults mounted aft. However, she was identical to the *Brooklyn*-class cruisers—built in the same years—except for armament and a few minor details. Overall length was 608 feet, original beam was 61 feet, displacement was 9,300 tons standard (13,000 plus when loaded for battle) and draft was 20 feet average (25 feet maximum.) Her top speed was just over 32 knots, horsepower was 100,000 and she had four shafts. With a fuel capacity of 2,243 tons Wichita could steam 7,200 miles at 15 knots or 3,300 miles at 25 knots.

Protection for *Wichita* demonstrated the continuing trend for more armor in both heavy and light cruisers. Side armor ranged from 1.5 inch fore and aft to 5 inches amidships, deck armor was 3 inches plus 2 inches, turret faces carried 5 to 6 inches with 3 inches on turret sides and backs, and the conning tower was defended by 8 inches of steel. Distribution of armor was continuous from beneath turret number one to turret number three with extensions vital to topside command and communication centers fore and aft. Beginning with *Wichita*, all heavy and light cruisers with scout planes would store two to four planes in the built-in fantail hangar. The planes would be launched from either of two catapults also located aft.

Armament for this cruiser followed the pattern for all post *Pensacola* heavy cruisers. The nine main armament 8-inch guns were placed in three triple turrets, two forward and one aft. Initial secondary armament consisted of eight 5-inch guns and eight .50-caliber machine guns. During the war the .50-caliber machine guns were replaced by twenty 40mm guns (two twins and four quads) and eighteen 20mm guns. Four of the 5-inch dual-purpose guns were housed in enclosed mounts, a heavy cruiser first.

Laid down 28 October 1935 at the Philadelphia Navy Yard, the cruiser was sponsored at her launch on 16 November 1937 by Mrs. William F. Weigester and was commissioned 16 February 1939. First commander was Capt. Thaddeus A. Thompson.

When war began in Europe, *Wichita* was still working out minor problems from her shakedown cruise in the Caribbean, but a month later she was active on Neutrality Patrol. By December 1941 she was a veteran ship with a well-trained crew. Operating out of Iceland in the first days of declared war, the cruiser encountered bad luck when on 15 January 1942 she was caught in a severe storm with winds up to 100 knots. After two other vessels bounced off her hull during the storm, the cruiser ran aground. She was repaired at the New York Navy Yard in February, and then the cruiser prepared to join a task force built around the carrier *Wasp* and new battleship *Washington* for duty in European waters. En route to Britain, the force was hit by another storm and the force admiral in *Washington* was washed overboard. As a result, command of the force was passed to Rear Adm. Robert C. Griffen aboard *Wichita*. From April 1942 until August 1942 the cruiser helped convoy ships to the Soviet Union.

In October 1942 *Wichita* steamed toward North Africa to participate in the November "Operation Torch." Off Casablanca the cruiser battled shore batteries and Vichy French warships, taking one 8-inch shell that wounded 14 men. After quick repairs in New York City the cruiser departed for the Pacific and arrived just in time to take part in the Rennell Island fight 29 January 1943 in which *Chicago* was lost. *Wichita* was very fortunate to emerge from this battle undamaged as she was hit by an aerial torpedo that failed to detonate.

In April 1943 the cruiser steamed to the Aleutians and was active there until August 1943. In January 1944 she supported the invasion of the Marshalls and from then until the end of the year she screened carriers and shelled enemy-held islands throughout the Pacific. Just before and during the October 1944 Battle of Leyte Gulf, *Wichita* helped shield the "cripple division" comprised of damaged *Houston* (CL-81) and *Canberra* (CA-70) and later helped complete the destruction of *Chiyoda* off Cape Engano by pouring 8-inch shells into the enemy carrier which had been damaged earlier by American carrier planes. Before leaving the area, *Wichita* teamed with several destroyers to sink Japanese destroyer *Hatsuzuki*. The cruiser missed the early 1945 Battle of Iwo Jima due to repairs, but was off Okinawa for the last major battle in the Pacific. After "Magic Carpet" duties in December 1945 and January 1946 the cruiser was decommissioned 3 February 1947 and was sold for scrap 14 August 1959.

Wichita at New York City 15 June 1939. Last of the "treaty" heavy cruisers, *Wichita* was greatly similar to the *Brooklyn*-class light cruisers. The major difference was armament. USN

Wichita with *Wasp* (CV-7) at Scapa Flow in April 1942. USN

THE BALTIMORE CLASS

THE APPROACH OF WAR IN EUROPE IN LATE 1939 AND German success in early 1940 spurred the U.S. Congress to pass legislation for military appropriations that overwhelmed earlier appropriation bills. Part of the 1940 naval expansion legislation called for a new class of heavy cruisers. These ships would be the first heavy cruisers to be built since World War I that would not be designed in accord with treaty promises; consequently, American naval designers and builders could concentrate on building warships that could meet the needs of the Navy instead of the desires of politicians.

The *Baltimore*-class cruisers would profit greatly by the design errors and limitations of the treaty cruisers. They would be larger by some 3,000 tons, would possess greater armor protection and would carry more anti-aircraft guns.

Originally the *Baltimore* class was to have 18 units. However, the 18th warship, *Northampton* (CA-125), was cancelled. Three of the ships would be sufficiently modified to unofficially constitute a separate class (*Oregon City* class—*Oregon City* [CA-122], *Albany* [CA-123] and *Rochester* [CA-124]). An additional seven members of the class (*Columbus* [CA-74], *Helena* [CA-75], *Bremerton* [CA-122], *Fall River* [CA-131], *Macon* [CA-132], *Toledo* [CA-133] and *Los Angeles* [CA-135]) were completed too late to earn any battle stars for World War II service and therefore are not detailed in this book.

None of the *Baltimores* were lost in World War II and damage incurred was relatively light. A major factor for this success was the late arrival of the cruisers in combat zones. Commendable service was rendered by the seven units of this class that did fight and as a class the *Baltimores* earned a total of 34 battle stars (*Baltimore* 9, *Boston* 10, *Canberra* 7, the second *Quincy* 4, *Pittsburgh* 2, *St. Paul* 1 and the second *Chicago* 1. Four members of the class that fought in World War II also distinguished themselves in later roles, which will be discussed elsewhere.

The average cost of the seven combat-active *Baltimores* was approximately $40 million. Their complement was slightly over 1,500 officers and men. They had a length of 673' 6" overall—considerably longer than earlier heavy cruisers. Beam was 70 feet and maximum draft was over 26 feet. Displacement was 13,600 tons standard and 16,400 tons when loaded for combat. Top speed was 33 knots, horsepower 120,000, and each ship had four shafts. Fuel capacity of 2,593 tons gave the *Baltimores* a range of 7,900 miles at 15 knots or 4,800 miles at 25 knots.

Protection for the *Baltimores* was the best of any American heavy cruisers to fight from 1941 through 1945. Side armor was 6 inches, deck armor was 3 inches plus 2 inches and turret faces carried 6-inch steel. The distribution of armor was extensive. Four float planes were carried in the fantail hangar and could be launched by either of two catapults. Unlike the *Wichita*, the *Baltimores* had twin aircraft cranes to serve the hangar and catapults.

The usual pattern of main armament for heavy cruisers was again utilized for this class. Three triple turrets, two fore and one aft, housed new 8-inch guns that fired a heavier shell than those carried by earlier cruisers. Secondary armament consisted of twelve 5-inch dual-purpose rifles, forty-eight 40mm barrels (12 quads) and twenty-two to twenty-eight 20mm weapons.

In appearance the *Baltimores* were distinct from other heavy cruisers but did resemble the *Cleveland*-class light cruisers. Still, the *Baltimores* would not be confused with the *Clevelands* primarily due to the unique shape of their bow, their twin aircraft cranes and the number of main battery turrets. Toward the end of the lives of several members of this class, appearance changed greatly. A few of these cruisers would change only with the addition of newer gun mounts or with the removal of catapults and one crane so they could accommodate helicopters instead of fixed wing planes; others would be completely rebuilt as the first series of guided missile cruisers.

BALTIMORE CA-68

(9 Battle Stars) *Baltimore* (CA-68), named for the city in Maryland, was laid down 26 May 1941 by the Bethlehem Steel Co. at Fore River, Mass. Sponsored by Mrs. Howard W. Jackson at the launch 28 July 1942, the cruiser was commissioned 15 April 1943 with Capt. W.C. Calhoun in command. A total building time of 23 months reflected the urgency of war; the average building time of the prewar treaty cruisers was approximately 38 months.

Unlike heavy cruisers before her, the *Baltimore* could devote little time to long shakedown cruises. With the

Pacific war about to see the major American push through Japanese-held islands to the home islands, *Baltimore* hastily completed trials and training and joined the Pacific Fleet in the fall of 1943. By the time *Baltimore* and her wartime sisters arrived in the Pacific, only one major surface action remained to be fought (Leyte Gulf, October 1944) and therefore the *Baltimores* would fulfill a primary role of screening carriers and supplying shore bombardment. *Baltimore* was particularly well suited for these two tasks and she proved her worth in the Marshalls, Gilberts, Carolines and Marianas. Just after the

Battle of the Philippine Sea (19-20 June 1944) the cruiser returned to the United States to carry President Roosevelt to Pearl Harbor to meet with Admiral Nimitz and General MacArthur. In August *Baltimore* carried the president to Alaska. Returning to combat operations in November 1944, the cruiser supported attacks on the Philippines and participated in the Iwo Jima operation and the Okinawa operation in early 1945. Never severely damaged, the class leader ended the war with the happy assignment of returning veterans to the United States.

Baltimore was placed out of commission in reserve 8 July 1946 but was recommissioned 28 November 1951 in response to the outbreak of war in Korea. Assigned to the Atlantic Fleet, the cruiser did not see action off Korea. In June 1953 *Baltimore* represented the United States Navy in the Coronation Naval Review to honor the new monarch, Queen Elizabeth II. After a brief deployment to the Pacific in 1955 the cruiser was again placed out of commission at Bremerton, Wash., 31 May 1956. She was stricken 15 February 1971 and scrapped.

Bow view of *Baltimore*, off Boston, Mass., 10 September 1943. The new cruiser had been in commission only five months when this photo was taken.   USN

Baltimore, first of the post-treaty heavy cruisers, off San Francisco 18 October 1944.   USN

President Roosevelt, Gen. Douglas MacArthur and Adm. Chester Nimitz on board *Baltimore* at Pearl Harbor 26 July 1944.   USN

(10 Battle Stars) Named for the coastal city in Massachusetts, Boston (CA-69) was laid down 30 June 1941 by the Bethlehem Steel Co., Fore River, Mass. Sponsored by Mrs. M.J. Tobin, the wife of the mayor of Boston, the ship was launched 26 August 1942 and was commissioned 30 June 1943 with Capt. J.H. Carson in command.

When Boston arrived at Pearl Harbor 6 December 1943 to begin her combat career she was already in some senses a veteran ship. When the Northampton was sunk off Tassafaronga in 1942 her surviving crewmembers were reassigned primarily to two new warships—battleships Iowa (BB-61) and Boston. The cruiser joined the fleet in time for the Marshall Islands campaign, and thereafter

Boston on a full-power run in October 1944.

USN

The first guided-missile cruiser in the U.S. Navy, Boston is seen here test firing a Terrier missile in 1956. The cruiser was converted between 1952 and 1955 for her new role.

USN

participated in the major operations of 1944 and 1945, missing only the invasions of Iwo Jima and Okinawa. When the Pacific war ended *Boston* was off the coast of Japan having bombarded the home islands in July and August 1945. On occupation duty until 28 February 1946, the ship was placed out of commission in reserve at Bremerton, Wash., on 12 March 1946.

In February 1952 *Boston* was reclassified CAG-1 guided missile heavy cruiser. Towed from Bremerton to the East Coast for conversion and modernization, *Boston* was recommissioned 1 November 1955 and with sister ship *Canberra* she became one of the first two guided missile cruisers in the world. The size of the beam-riding Terrier missile, nearly 30 feet long and weighing a ton

and a half, required a fairly large ship with speed adequate to defend fast carriers. During conversion the aft 8-inch turret was removed to make room for the missile launchers but the two forward 8-inch turrets were retained. Ironically, when both *Boston* and *Canberra* became obsolete in the late 1960s because of newer, more effective missiles for fleet defense, they were found to be worthy of continued use for shore bombardment off Vietnam. After reverting to her original hull number in May 1968, *Boston* was finally retired after 28 years of excellent service to her country. The cruiser was decommissioned 5 May 1970, stricken 1 November 1973, and sold for scrap.

CANBERRA CA-70

Canberra in drydock after being hit by an aerial torpedo 13 October 1944. Twenty-three men were killed and damage was sufficiently severe to require a two-week tow to safety. USN

(7 Battle Stars) The *Canberra* honored the capital city of Australia and the Australian heavy cruiser that was sunk along with the *Astoria*, the *Quincy* and the *Vincennes* during the Battle of Savo Island. *Canberra* (CA-70) was laid down 3 September 1941, and at her launch 19 April 1943 the cruiser was sponsored by Lady Alice C. Dixon. On 14 October 1943 the ship was commissioned with Capt. A.R. Early in command.

Canberra arrived in the Pacific in time to participate in the latter stages of the Marshall Islands invasion (February 1944). Like her two earlier sister ships, she assumed the primary role of carrier defense. In March and April the cruiser supported carrier raids in the Carolines and after raids on Marcus Island and Wake Island in May, *Canberra* steamed to cover the June invasion of the Marianas. With TF 38 in October *Canberra* screened carriers while they delivered air strikes against enemy bases on Formosa and Okinawa in preparation for the invasion of the Philippines. Late on 13 October during this operation *Canberra* was hit by an aerial torpedo. Twenty-three men were killed and both engine rooms were flooded. The ship was dead in the water less than 100 miles off enemy held Formosa, and prospects did not appear overly favorable to save her. The following afternoon another enemy air attack succeeded in placing a torpedo into *Houston* (CL-81) which had been sent to reinforce the group covering *Canberra*'s withdrawal. Now, two American cruisers were unable to move under their own power. Attempting to turn a bad situation into a profit, Admiral Halsey hoped to lure the Japanese Fleet toward "Bait Division One" and then overwhelm the enemy surface units with air power. However, the Japanese recognized the ruse and aborted their sortie. On the 16th the retiring American ships underwent another air attack and *Houston* took another torpedo. On the 27th both damaged cruisers arrived at Ulithi. After temporary repairs at Manus the ship moved on to Boston for permanent repairs. For *Canberra* World War II was over.

Returning to the West Coast in late 1945, *Canberra* was placed out of commission at Bremerton 7 March 1947, but in January 1952 she was reclassified CAG-2 and she joined sister ship *Boston* on the East Coast for modernization and conversion to a guided-missile cruiser. Recommissioned 15 June 1956, the cruiser served in her new role until decommissioned 16 February 1970. On 31 July 1978 she was sold for scrap after an effort to preserve her as a memorial failed.

QUINCY CA-71

(4 Battle Stars) *Quincy* (CA-71) began life under the name *St. Paul* when she was laid down at Bethlehem Steel Co.'s Shipbuilding Division in Quincy, Mass., on 9 October 1941. However, the name was changed 16 October 1942 to perpetuate the memory of *Quincy* (CA-39) which was sunk during the August 1942 Battle of Savo Island. The new cruiser was launched 23 June 1943 and was sponsored by Mrs. Henry S. Morgan—a daughter of the famed Civil War-era diplomat Charles Francis Adams—who had earlier sponsored *Quincy* (CA-39). Commissioned 10 October 1944 under the command of Capt. Elliot M. Senn, the cruiser departed immediately for a shakedown cruise to the Caribbean.

First combat action for the new warship came on 6 June 1944, D-Day in Europe, when she stood off Utah Beach to engage enemy shore batteries. Bombardment continued through 17 June with the cruiser contributing greatly to the reduction of enemy strength. Later in the month *Quincy* was off Cherbourg to silence German batteries there. In July the cruiser steamed to the Mediterranean for brief training off Sicily and Malta and on 15 August *Quincy* was a member of an Allied force providing fire support to cover the invasion of southern France.

On 23 January 1945 President Roosevelt and other dignitaries embarked on *Quincy* for a voyage to Malta, the first stop for the president en route to the Yalta Conference in February. After flying on to the conference with Churchill and Stalin, the president returned to *Quincy* and on 27 February 1944 the cruiser arrived at Newport News, Va. Her service to the diplomatic theater of war completed, *Quincy* was ordered to the Pacific and on 16 April the cruiser joined Allied units off Okinawa to screen carriers. In May the cruiser was off Kyushu, one of the four major islands of the Japanese homeland, to screen carriers during their raids. These raids continued until the war's end three months later.

After a period serving as part of the occupation force in Japan, the cruiser returned to Bremerton where she was decommissioned 19 October 1946. On 31 January 1952 *Quincy* was recommissioned for service off Korea but arrived just as that conflict ended in the summer of 1953. Decommissioned again on 2 July 1954 at Bremerton, the cruiser remained in mothballs until stricken 1 October 1973 and sold for scrap.

Port-quarter view of the second *Quincy* (CA-71), near Boston, 15 December 1943.　　　　USN

PITTSBURGH CA-72

(2 Battle Stars) Originally named Albany, *Pittsburgh* (CA-72) was laid down on 3 February 1943 by the Bethlehem Steel Co., Quincy, Mass. Sponsored by Mrs. Cornelius D. Scully, wife of the mayor of Pittsburgh, Pa., the ship was launched 22 February 1944 and was commissioned 10 October 1944. *Pittsburgh*'s first captain, John Gingrich, would remain with the cruiser through her most difficult days in combat.

Although commissioned with less than a year of war remaining in the Pacific, *Pittsburgh* would see her share of action and render commendable service. First combat for the cruiser came off Iwo Jima in February 1945 as she provided gunfire support and air defense. While the cruiser was screening carriers on 19 March during air raids on the Japanese homeland the carrier *Franklin* (CV-13) was severely damaged. With casualties of 724 dead and 265 wounded, with power lost and within easy range of enemy air bases, *Franklin*'s survival chances were in doubt. The *Pittsburgh* collected three dozen *Franklin* crewmen from the water, and then the cruiser began towing the fiercely burning carrier toward safety. During the slow movement away from danger the cruiser had to continue air defense, twice fighting off air attacks against the highly visible burning carrier. *Pittsburgh* con-

tinued the tow until the following day when the *Franklin* surprisingly came to life and began to move under her own power. For two full days and nights Captain Gingrich refused to leave the bridge until attacks ceased and *Franklin* was well on her way to safety.

In April 1945 *Pittsburgh* was off Okinawa screening carriers, providing shore bombardment, and using her spotter planes for the rescue of downed carrier pilots. On 4 June the cruiser turned from one enemy to another as the threat of Japanese planes and submarines was temporarily replaced by that of a typhoon. On the 5th winds of over 70 knots and 100-foot waves contributed to the buckling of the second deck and consequent loss of the bow back to the number one 8-inch turret. In the continuing storm, the cruiser had to fight flooding, hold her position against the wind and waves, and manuever to miss the still-floating bow section. When the storm's fury subsided the cruiser proceeded slowly toward Guam. The bow structure, nicknamed "McKeesport" after a suburb of the city of Pittsburgh, was also salvaged and happily no lives were lost in its severance. Sporting a false bow, the cruiser steamed to Bremerton for repair and was there when the war concluded.

Pittsburgh was decommissioned 7 March 1947 but was

recommissioned 25 September 1951. During the Korean War the cruiser operated in the Atlantic and Mediterranean. Final service was rendered in the Far East in late 1954 and early 1955 when the cruiser covered the Chinese Nationalists defense of the Tachen Islands. Decommissioned again at Bremerton 28 August 1956, *Pittsburgh* was stricken 1 July 1973 and scrapped.

On 5 June 1945 *Pittsburgh* lost her bow in a typhoon. Despite the damage, no lives were lost. NA

ST. PAUL CA-73

(1 Battle Star for World War II, 8 Battle Stars for Korean War, 8 Battle Stars for Vietnam) *St. Paul* (CA-73) won only one battle star for World War II service but she became quite well known for her combat service off Korea and Vietnam. Before this famous cruiser was towed away to be scrapped in 1980 she earned eight battle stars for service off Korea and eight more for action off Vietnam. At the close of her life she had garnered a total of 17 battle stars in three wars and was awarded the Navy Unit Commendation for her performance during the Vietnam conflict.

Beginning life as *Rochester*, the cruiser was laid down on 3 February 1943 at Bethelhem Steel Co. in Quincy, Mass. Sponsored by Mrs. John J. McDonough at the launch on 16 September 1944, *St. Paul*, named for the capital of Minnesota, was commissioned 17 February 1945 with Capt. E.H. von Heimburg in command.

By the time *St. Paul* arrived for duty in the Pacific only one campaign appeared to remain—the invasion of Japan. In July and August 1945 *St. Paul* helped screen carriers as their planes struck the enemy home islands. The cruiser also bombarded industrial targets on 29 July and 9 August. On 15 August 1945 offensive operations ceased as preparations began for the surrender ceremony on 2 September in Tokyo Bay. *St. Paul* was present for these formalities. After the surrender, the cruiser remained in Japanese waters for occupation duty. Unlike the earlier sisters of her class she was not decommissioned in the years between the end of World War II and the opening of the Korean War in June 1950.

When war began in Korea, *St. Paul* hurried from the eastern Pacific to the Far East. Except for brief periods of repair and maintenance *St. Paul* fought from the beginning to the end of the Korean War. Constantly on the gun line, she dueled shore batteries at Inchon and numerous other locations at close range. When not shelling enemy gun positions, transportation arteries or troop concentrations, she helped screen carriers. She was hit once without major injury to ship or personnel, and her worst experience was the loss of 30 men when a fire broke out in number one turret on 21 April 1952. It is believed that this cruiser fired the last salvo from a major surface unit just before the truce in Korea (27 July 1953) and just before the surrender of Japan in 1945.

After the Korean War *St. Paul* operated with the Seventh Fleet in the Far East and was at sea when Quemoy was threatened by Communist China in 1954–1955. In the summer of 1959 the cruiser became the first major U.S. Navy ship to be based in the Far East since

before World War II. Based in Japan, she and her men were popular with the Japanese and numerous cultural and humanitarian services were rendered, and received, during the next three years. From 1965 until 1970 *St. Paul* provided gunfire support off Vietnam. The cruiser was hit once but no one was killed.

From 30 April 1971, when she was decommissioned, until early 1980 *St. Paul* rested and rusted at Bremerton. Towed to San Pedro, Calif., the veteran cruiser of three wars was scrapped in the summer of 1980.

CHICAGO CA-136

(1 Battle Star) When the first cruiser (CA-29) named for the great city in Illinois was launched the people of that city were not particularly overwhelmed with joy and pride. However, when that vessel was lost off Rennell Island in January 1943 they were so upset that they bought $40 million worth of war bonds to have a proposed *Baltimore*-class cruiser carry on the name. The *Chicago* (CA-136) was laid down 28 July 1943. The other cruisers in her class that won battle stars were laid down at Quincy, Mass., but *Chicago* was built at the Philadelphia Navy Yard. At the ship's launch on 20 August 1944 Mrs. E.J. Kelly, wife of Chicago's mayor, christened the vessel. With Capt. R. Hartung in command the cruiser was commissioned 10 January 1945 and arrived off the coast of Japan in July to support carrier strikes and bombard the home islands. After occupation duty in 1946 the

cruiser was placed out of commission 6 June 1947.

After a lengthy period in mothballs, *Chicago* was reclassified as CG-11 on 1 November 1958. In 1959 the conversion process to a guided-missile cruiser began and the ship, new from the third deck up, was recommissioned in May 1964. In this capacity the cruiser served until decommissioned 1 March 1980. The highlight of her career occurred during the Vietnam War as her aircraft direction equipment was used to direct fighters to intercept enemy planes. One of her Talos missiles also shot down an approaching North Vietnamese plane 50 miles away and her missiles often were used to destroy enemy radar installations. Currently (1983) mothballed at Bremerton, her fate is unknown as a group of citizens in Chicago are attempting to raise funds to preserve the ship as a museum at the city's Navy Pier.

The second *Chicago* (CA-136) seen here soon after her 10 January 1945 commissioning. Note OS2U Kingfishers on catapults.
USN

Chicago, newly designated CG-11, undergoing conversion at San Francisco in 1961 to become a guided-missile cruiser. USN

Too late to participate in World War II, the second *Helena*, seen here saluting President Truman at the October 1945 Navy Day celebration, compiled an admirable record off Korea with four battle stars and the award of the Presidential Unit Citation. USN

ALASKA
CLASS
BATTLECRUISERS

THE ALASKA CLASS "BATTLECRUISERS"

THE CONGRESSIONAL LEGISLATION OF 1940 authorized warships of all classes, but probably none of the authorizations were any more unique than the six-ship class of large cruisers (official designation), more often referred to as "battlecruisers." By 1940 several fast German pocket battleships carrying 11-inch guns had caused alarm in Allied navies and there was a concern that a similar class was being constructed by Japan. Although the Japanese were not building such a class, the United States Navy felt a need to respond to the potential threat in the Pacific and known threat in the Atlantic.

Response to the Axis threat was the *Alaska*-class authorization in July 1940 of six ships (*Alaska* [CB-1], *Guam* [CB-2], *Hawaii* [CB-3], *Philippines* [CB-4], *Puerto Rico* [CB-5] and *Samoa* [CB-6]). The last three (CBs 4-6) were ordered but were cancelled three years later. *Hawaii* (CB-3) was 84-percent complete when the war ended but was never finished and was sold for scrap in 1959. *Alaska* and *Guam*, however, would be commissioned in time to serve and earn three and two battle stars respectively. Although the recipients of adverse reviews by some naval authorities and historians, the *Alaskas* did fill the void between the slow, pre-1940s, big-gun battleships and fast, small-gunned cruisers. In theory the *Alaskas* could defeat any other cruiser thanks to their heavier armor and larger guns, and could race away from slower battleships that could outgun them. By the time the two *Alaskas* that did see combat were commissioned, the character of the Pacific war was such that the functions of the ships were limited to air defense for carriers and shore bombardment. In these roles the ships were superb but not unique. History might have recorded a more glowing report of these ships if they had been available in time to protect the few American carriers struggling to defend Guadalcanal or meet the "Tokyo Express" in 1942-1943.

The cost of a completed *Alaska* was approximately $70 million. With a complement of 2,200 and a propensity to consume fuel at a high rate, the *Alaskas* were not the most cost-efficient vessels in the Navy. The members of this class were considerably larger than both the earlier cruisers and the contemporary *Baltimores* at 808 feet in overall length. Beam was 91 feet, draft was 32 feet maximum and displacement was 27,500 tons standard and 34,000 plus when loaded for combat. Top speed on trials was 31 knots (two knots slower than design), horsepower was 150,000 and each ship had four shafts. Fuel capacity was 3,710 tons and range was in excess of 7,000 miles at 15 knots.

Protection for the *Alaskas* was quite respectable. Side armor ranged from 5 inches to 9 inches, deck armor was 3.75 inches plus 4.25 inches and turret faces carried steel 12.75 inches thick. The distribution of armor was more in keeping with the selectivity characterizing cruisers as opposed to the trend in battleships. Four float planes could be carried and were launched from two catapults amidships, a throwback to early treaty cruisers and a definite design quirk in view of the fact that contemporary battleships, heavy cruisers, and light cruisers were being built with aircraft functions at the stern.

Main armament for the class consisted of nine 12-inch rifles in three triple turrets, two forward and one aft. Secondary armament featured twelve 5-inch dual purpose guns, fifty-six 40mm barrels (14 quad mounts) and thirty-four 20mm Oerlikons.

ALASKA CB-1

(3 Battle Stars) Named for a territory that would become a state 3 January 1959, *Alaska* was laid down by the New York Shipbuilding Corp. on 16 December 1941. Sponsored by Mrs. Ernest Gruening at the launch 15 August 1943, the ship was commissioned 17 June 1944 with Capt. P.K. Fischler in command.

The new cruiser joined the Pacific Fleet 13 January 1945 and spent the next seven months screening carriers, supporting the invasions of Iwo Jima and Okinawa, attacking enemy shipping in the East China Sea and participating in operations against the Japanese home islands. After the war the cruiser remained in the Far East supporting occupation forces. *Alaska* returned to the United States in December 1945 and was placed out of commission at Bayonne, N.J., 17 February 1947. Never returning to active service, the cruiser was sold for scrap in July 1961.

Alaska off Philadelphia on 30 July 1944, two weeks after the new battlecruiser (large cruiser, officially) was commissioned.   USN

Alaska alongside the battleship *Missouri* (bottom) in 1944. At the upper right is light carrier *Cowpens*.   NA

GUAM CB-2

(2 Battle Stars) Named for an island in the Marianas group, *Guam* (CB-2) was laid down 2 February 1942 by the New York Shipbuilding Corp. Mrs. G.J. McMillan christened the ship at launch 12 November 1943, and *Guam* was commissioned 17 September 1944 with Capt. Leland P. Lovette in command.

In the spring of 1945 American forces invaded Okinawa and began consistent raids on the Japanese home islands. Now within range of Japanese bombers and kamikazes, the U.S. Navy absorbed terrific damage.

When *Guam* reported for duty in March 1945 she was quite welcome. No doubt her one incomplete sister, *Hawaii*, and the three cancelled cruisers of the class would have been warmly greeted by the fleet had they too been available.

Guam saw five months of heavy action before the Pacific War ended. After brief occupation duty the cruiser steamed for San Francisco. On 17 February 1947 the ship was decommissioned at Bayonne, New Jersey, and was sold for scrap 24 May 1961.

Guam off Trinidad in late 1944 while conducting main battery gunnery practice.   USN

Port-side view of *Guam* off Trinidad, 13 November 1944.   USN

The 84-percent-complete *Hawaii* being towed away for scrapping 20 June 1959.

USN

LIGHT
CRUISERS

LIGHT CRUISERS

LIGHT CRUISERS WERE NOT BUILT TO ABSORB severe damage; their functions reflected this characteristic. Although use of the term "light cruiser" did not have official sanction and designation (CL) until 1 January 1931, which was the effective date of the Treaty of London, the terminology was applied to smaller cruisers before 1931. A light cruiser first and foremost was a fast ship assigned duties as a raider, a scout for the battle fleet, and a destroyer flotilla leader. Relatively inexpensive ships, their functions expanded in the 1930s when carrier planes and cruiser-borne float planes assumed the function of scouting. By 1941 light cruisers were serving as anti-aircraft platforms, shore bombardment vessels, and convoy escorts. In surface combat it was expected that the U.S. Navy's prewar light cruisers would counter enemy destroyers and light cruisers, but on several memorable occasions they had to fire their 6-inch and 5-inch shells at battleships and heavy cruisers. Though never a match for battleships, the later classes of American light cruisers with their improved armor and rapid fire 6-inch guns were felt to be the equal of enemy heavy cruisers.

During the course of World War II 47 American light cruisers earned one or more battle stars. Of these 17 were in commission on 7 December 1941. When the war ended only three (*Atlanta* (CL-51), *Juneau* (CL-52) and *Helena* (CL-50) had been lost to enemy action with the major factor in the sinkings being the torpedo. Of the seven heavy cruisers and three light cruisers lost by the United States Navy in World War II, all were hit by torpedoes. Aerial torpedoes killed *Chicago*, submarine torpedoes killed *Indianapolis* and *Juneau* while destroyer-launched torpedoes killed the others.

Four distinct classes of American light cruisers were active during World War II. Some of the ships of two of the classes sported minor charges. These offshoots are generally treated as separate classes but will be combined in this writing. Therefore, the classes of American light cruisers to fight were the *Omaha* class; the *Brooklyn-Helena* class; the *Atlanta-Oakland* class; and the *Cleveland* class. The old World War I-era *Omaha* class had 10 members but only eight won battle stars. The fine *Brooklyn* class had seven members, all of which won battle stars, and its two-member derivative class—the *Helenas*—earned battle stars. The *Atlanta* class had four battle-star-earning members and the derivative *Oakland* class also had four battle-star-winning units. Finally, the post-treaty *Cleveland* class produced 29 members of which 22 earned battle stars. The *Cleveland* class also supplied nine additional hulls that were converted into the highly successful *Independence* class of fast, light carriers (CVLs) which all earned battle stars.

THE OMAHA CLASS

AUTHORIZED IN 1916 BEFORE THE UNITED STATES entered World War I, none of the members of this class were completed before the end of "the war to end all wars" in 1918. Ten units of this class were ordered (*Omaha* [CL-4], *Milwaukee* [CL-5], *Cincinnati* [CL-6], *Raleigh* [CL-7], *Detroit* [CL-8], *Richmond* [CL-9], *Concord* [CL-10], *Trenton* [CL-11], *Marblehead* [CL-12] and *Memphis* [CL-13]) but two would not earn battle stars in World War II. *Milwaukee* was loaned to the Russian Navy and *Memphis* did not enter combat. Due to their age (a cruiser's expected service life was 20 years and all the *Omahas* were nearing that figure when World War II began), and because of their paucity of armor and unfortunate main armament placement, these cruisers were for the most part not assigned to frontline duty. Consequently, the entire class earned only 17 battle stars. Still, this class served admirably in all theaters of combat with battle stars earned as follows: *Detroit* 6, *Raleigh* 3, *Marblehead* and *Richmond* 2 each, *Omaha*, *Cincinnati*, *Trenton* and *Concord* one each.

Under construction when the 1922 Washington Naval Conference convened, these ships were little affected by the results of the conference. Costing approximately $6.5 million each, the *Omahas* maintained a prewar complement of 458 officers and men and 675 in wartime. Overall length was 555 feet with a beam of 55 feet. Displacement was 7,050 tons standard and 9,700 tons when ready for combat while draft ranged from 13 to 17 feet. Designed to achieve 35 knots, the ships could operate near 30 knots when loaded. Horsepower for this class was 90,000. Each vessel had four screws and carried 1,986 tons of fuel, which provided a cruising radius of 3,100 miles at 25 knots or 6,800 miles at 15 knots.

Protection for the *Omahas* centered more on their speed than on armor. Side armor was only 3 inches and deck armor was only 1.5-inch. Originally built without catapults, several members of the class had them installed later to operate two float planes. Armament was not consistent throughout the class. *Detroit* entered the war with eight 6-inch guns, *Concord*, *Omaha* and *Tren-*

ton carried 12 while *Cincinnati, Raleigh, Richmond* and *Marblehead* mounted 10. The 6-inch, main-armament guns were mounted in single barbettes with one twin mount forward and one aft emphasizing end-on gunfire at the expense of using all main armament for broadsides. Early anti-aircraft protection was provided by six to eight 3-inch guns and .50-caliber machine guns. During wartime refits, 40mm and 20mm weapons were added but not in the great numbers that characterized the modernizations of later light cruisers. These vessels also carried six to ten 21-inch, above-water torpedo tubes for much of their careers.

In appearance the *Omahas* could not be mistaken for any other class of light cruisers. Their four stacks distinguished them from all light and heavy cruisers. Overage and considerably obsolete at the end of the war, all units were quickly decommissioned and sold for scrap. They had been constantly in service from their commissioning dates and they had served well in training men who would eventually fight aboard newer cruisers. They had also served in combat roles.

OMAHA CL-4

(**1 Battle Star**) Named for the city in Nebraska, *Omaha* (CL-4) was laid down 6 December 1918 by the Todd Shipbuilding and Drydock Co. of Tacoma, Wash. The cruiser was sponsored at her launch on 14 December 1920 by Miss Louise B. White and was commissioned 24 February 1923 with Capt. David C. Hanrahan commanding.

Omaha spent the vast majority of her prewar career in the Atlantic. Just before the Pacific War broke the cruiser got a taste of events to come. On 6 November 1941 while on Neutrality Patrol *Omaha* and destroyer *Somers* (DD-381) encountered the German freighter *Odenwald*, which was flying the American flag to hide her true identity. When challenged by *Omaha* the German crew attempted to sink their ship with explosives. However, the boarding crew from *Omaha* disdained the obvious danger of entering a sabotaged ship and managed to save the vessel. After the United States officially entered the war, *Omaha* continued her patrol duties in the South Atlantic. On 4-5 January 1944 the cruiser found German blockade runners. The enemy ship sighted on 4 January was scuttled and the ship encountered on the 5th was sunk by gunfire after the Germans had set fire to their vessel. Both ships were carrying rubber, a commodity in great demand by all the countries at war.

In March 1944 the cruiser reported to Naples in preparation for Allied landings in southern France. In August she protected the flank of warships bombarding Toulon, later joined the bombardment herself and was part of the force that captured the island of Porquerolles. Returning to patrol duties in the South Atlantic after the southern France operation, the cruiser remained in the South Atlantic until the end of the war. Decommissioned 1 November 1945, the old, much-used cruiser was stricken 28 November 1945 and sold to be scrapped in February 1946.

Omaha (at right) just after her boarding party had entered the German freighter *Odenwald* on 6 November 1941.
                                                                                    USN

German blockade runner *Burgenland* being scuttled by her crew after she was intercepted in the South Atlantic by *Omaha* in January 1944.   USN

CINCINNATI CL-6

(1 Battle Star) Named for the city in Ohio, *Cincinnati* (CL-6) was laid down 15 May 1920. The cruiser was sponsored at her launch by Mrs. C.E. Tudor on 23 May 1921 at the Todd Dry Dock Co., Tacoma, Wash., and the ship was commissioned 1 January 1924 with Capt. C.P. Nelson commanding.

Much-traveled throughout the Pacific and Atlantic before World War II, *Cincinnati* left the Pacific in March 1941 for the last time. Assigned to Neutrality Patrol duties in the Atlantic, the cruiser continued patrols and convoy escort assignments after 7 December 1941. She searched constantly for German blockade runners, and *Cincinnati* was part of a force that intercepted the *SS Annaliese Essberger* on 21 November 1942, taking 62 prisoners. After an early 1944 overhaul, the cruiser escorted convoys from New York to Northern Ireland, patrolled the Mediterranean during the invasion of southern France and spent the remainder of the European war patrolling shipping lanes in the South Atlantic. In the summer of 1945 the cruiser carried midshipmen on two training cruises. Decommissioned 1 November 1945, the ship was sold for scrap 27 February 1946.

Cincinnati seen here soon after her 1 January 1924 commissioning.   USN

(3 Battle Stars) Seldom do pictorial accounts of the bombing of Pearl Harbor appear without a photo of *Raleigh* listing heavily and fighting for life. And, like other wounded survivors of that attack, *Raleigh* would in the following four years give the Japanese reason for regret for not totally destroying the unprepared American warships sitting at Pearl.

Named for the city in North Carolina, *Raleigh* (CL-7) was laid down at the Bethlehem Steel Co. of Quincy, Mass., on 16 August 1920. Sponsored by Miss Jennie Proctor at the launch 25 October 1922, *Raleigh* was commissioned 6 February 1924. The ship's first captain was William C. Watts.

In February and March 1927 *Raleigh* carried United States Marines to Nicaragua and stood off the coast to render further assistance if required. (Half a century later American naval units steam off the coast of this same Central American country hoping intervention will not be necessary as yet another generation of Nicaraguans search for their national soul and for domestic tranquility.)

The *Raleigh* was based primarily in the Pacific after August 1933. *Raleigh* steamed to Norfolk, Va., in the summer of 1936 and after repairs she became a part of a force ordered to evacuate Americans and others from Spain as that country was being ravaged by civil war. This "temporary" duty in Spanish waters lasted over a year and the cruiser did not finally return to the Pacific until the fall of 1939.

On Sunday morning 7 December 1941 *Raleigh* was one of the first warships to be damaged in the infamous raid. Hit by an aerial torpedo amidships on the port side, the cruiser listed heavily. There was genuine concern that she might capsize. Behind her the old battleship *Utah* had turned over. However, *Raleigh*'s crew quickly counterflooded, jettisoned topside weight and ran additional lines to mooring floats. Later in the attack a bomb passed completely through the ship rendering minimal damage. *Raleigh*'s guns contributed to the destruction of several enemy planes, and, despite her damage, the salvage of the ship and her anti-aircraft defense made this day the proudest of her career.

Repairs and convoy-escort duty occupied most of 1942 for *Raleigh* but in November 1942 she began duty in the Aleutians that would occupy her on and off until February 1944. During these many months she escorted convoys, searched for Japanese ships, covered landings, and patrolled and provided bombardment support. Her service to the United States concluded with midshipmen training cruises to the Caribbean. Decommissioned 2 November 1945, *Raleigh* was sold for scrap 27 February 1946.

Raleigh in San Diego harbor 21 October 1933.   USN

Raleigh listing to port as a result of a Japanese aerial torpedo in Pearl Harbor 7 December 1941. In the background is the capsized *Utah*.   USN

DETROIT CL-8

(6 Battle Stars) Named for the city in Michigan, *Detroit* (CL-8) was laid down 10 November 1920 at Bethlehem Shipbuilding of Quincy, Mass. Sponsored by Miss M. Couzens at the launch 29 June 1922, the cruiser was commissioned 31 July 1923 with Capt. J. Halligan Jr. commanding.

Alongside sister ship *Raleigh* during the Nicaraguan crisis in 1927, *Detroit* in the same year transported Secretary of State F.B. Kellogg to the negotiations that led to the Kellogg-Briand peace pact. She divided her prewar service between the Atlantic and Pacific. The cruiser was based in the Pacific during the last years of peace and was in Pearl

Detroit in San Diego harbor 10 January 1935. *Detroit* garnered more battle stars (six) than any other unit of the *Omaha* class.   USN

Harbor when the Japanese struck. Undamaged in the raid, *Detroit* began her wartime experience by searching the coast of Oahu for possible enemy landings.

Like *Raleigh*, *Detroit* was occupied for most of 1942 in convoy-escort duty. In November 1942 she began operations in the Aleutians and remained in that region until after assaults in the northern Kuriles in the summer of 1944. Often supplying shore bombardment, the cruiser won battle stars in the Northern Pacific, off Iwo Jima and Okinawa.

After patrolling the west coast of South America for three months, the cruiser joined the Fifth Fleet at Ulithi 4 February 1945 as flagship for the replenishment group serving the fast-carrier task forces. Serving in this capacity until the Japanese surrender, she entered Tokyo Bay 1 September 1945 and directed replenishment operations for the occupation fleet. She returned veterans to the United States on her final voyage and was decommissioned 11 January 1946. The *Detroit* was sold for scrap 27 February 1946.

RICHMOND CL-9

(2 Battle Stars) Named for the capital of Virginia, *Richmond* (CL-9) was laid down 16 February 1920 by William Cramp and Sons in Philadelphia, Pa. She was sponsored by Miss Elizabeth S. Scott at the launch 29 September 1921, and was commissioned 2 July 1923 with Capt. David F. Boyd in command.

Early service was rendered by *Richmond* in 1924 by rescuing survivors of the *Tacoma*, which had wrecked on a reef. Alternating between the Pacific and Atlantic, the cruiser was patrolling the west coast of South America when war began between the United States and Japan. After convoy-escort duty and an overhaul, *Richmond* arrived in the Aleutians in January 1943. *Richmond* was part of a force comprised of one heavy cruiser (*Salt Lake City*) and four destroyers in March 1943 when the ene-

my attempted to break through to supply its garrisons on Attu and Kiska. Although outgunned by the enemy force of two heavy cruisers as well as two light cruisers and five destroyers, the American force chose battle. The ensuing fight is remembered as the Battle of the Komandorski Islands (see *Salt Lake City* for details). *Richmond* emerged from this action undamaged and had the pleasure of seeing the Japanese retire from the battle just as it seemed they would be victorious. Failure to land supplies and troops led to the eventual Japanese withdrawal of the two garrisons four months later. Patrol duties and bombardment of the northern Kuriles occupied *Richmond* for the remainder of the war. Decommissioned 21 December 1945, the cruiser was sold 18 December 1946.

Richmond is shown here in a full-power run in the 1920s. During the March 1943 Battle of the Komandorski Islands, *Richmond* helped turn back a superior Japanese force.   USN

CONCORD CL-10

(1 Battle Star) Named for the city in Massachusetts where one of the first two battles of the American Revolution was fought, *Concord* (CL-10) was laid down 29 March 1920 at Philadelphia, Pa., by William Cramp and Sons. Mrs. H. Butterick sponsored the ship at launching ceremonies 15 December 1921 and the cruiser was commissioned 3 November 1923 with Capt. O.G. Murfin commanding.

Having trained in both the Atlantic and Pacific in the years prior to war, *Concord* was preparing for overhaul when war began in 1941. Ready for service in February 1942, her initial duties centered on convoy escort to the Society Islands. From 5 September to 24 November 1943 she carried Rear Adm. R.E. Byrd into the southeast Pacific islands so the admiral could survey various islands for potential military and commercial use. While so engaged the cruiser suffered an internal gasoline explosion that killed 22 men. After repairs in March 1944 *Concord* joined the Northern Pacific Force on 2 April and participated in the bombardment of the Kuriles and disruption of Japanese shipping in that area. The cruiser was still operating in the Aleutians and Kuriles when the war ended. After covering occupation landings at Ominato, Japan, in September 1945 she steamed to Philadelphia where she was decommissioned 12 December 1945 and sold for scrap 21 January 1947.

TRENTON CL-11

(1 Battle Star) Named for the city in New Jersey and the site of George Washington's first significant victory in the Revolutionary War, *Trenton* (CL-11) was laid down 18 August 1920 at Philadelphia, Pa. by William Cramp and Sons. Sponsored by Miss Katherine E. Donnelly at the launch 19 April 1924, the new cruiser was commissioned 19 April 1924. First commanding officer was Capt. Edward C. Kalbfus.

Trenton's prewar career was sprinkled with notable assignments and events. After a serious fire in 1924 which killed or wounded everyone in number one turret, the cruiser carried special observer-mediator Col. Henry L. Stimson to Nicaragua in 1927. The cruiser was part of the force that protected American interests during the Spanish Civil War and was the vessel that carried the royal family of Luxembourg to the United States in July 1940 after the family had been forced to leave by advancing German troops.

After convoy escort duty and patrolling assignments in the first years of the war, *Trenton* arrived in the Aleutians in September 1944. Until August of 1945 the cruiser patrolled Alaskan waters, joined in bombardment raids on the Kuriles and conducted anti-shipping sweeps in the central Kuriles. Placed out of commission 20 December 1945, *Trenton* was sold for scrap 29 December 1946.

MARBLEHEAD CL-12

(2 Battle Stars, Navy Unit Commendation) The subject of one of the great dramas of World War II, *Marblehead* (CL-12), named for a port in Massachusetts, was laid down 4 August 1920 at Philadelphia, Pa., by William Cramp and Sons. Sponsored by Mrs. Joseph Evans at the launch 9 October 1923, the cruiser was commissioned 8 September 1924 with Capt. Chauncey Shackford commanding.

Like most of her sister ships *Marblehead* operated in both the Atlantic and Pacific before the war. She was part of the Pacific Fleet from 1933 to 1938 and was assigned to the Asiatic Fleet in January 1938. Based in the Philippines, *Marblehead* joined warships of the Royal Netherlands Navy and Royal Australian Navy to defend the Netherlands East Indies in the first days of war. Operating without sufficient air cover and with the difficulties inherent in a quickly assembled multinational force, *Marblehead* helped screen allied shipping and participated in attacks on Japanese convoys moving into the region.

On 4 February 1942 *Marblehead*'s force was attacked by Japanese planes. Heavy cruiser *Houston* was alongside and took one damaging hit. *Marblehead* took two direct hits, one amidships and one aft. Another bomb just missed the bow but was close enough to rupture plates and cause flooding. Over a dozen men were killed and nearly 70 had wounds of varying severity. The ship itself was in danger of being lost.

Fires were put out with difficulty, and the ship was down 12 degrees at the bow and listing. Only the amidships section of the cruiser was buoyant and it too was damaged. Bulkheads were torn, the hull greatly weakened, navigation and communication essentials destroyed and the rudder was locked causing the ship to circle to port. With the ship still under attack, full attention could not be given to damage control until later in the day. After surveying damage Capt. Arthur Robinson decided not to abandon although the ship was in obvious danger of breaking up in anything other than a calm sea. Too, there was fear that firing the 6-inch guns could place too great a strain on the weakened hull.

Marblehead steamed at moderate speed to Tjilatjap on the coast of Java using her engines to steer as the rudder was now locked by chains in an amidships position. However, the dock there was too small to allow the cruiser to patch her holes and drain her compartments. Also, Dutch authorities were anxious for the cruiser to leave as they feared her presence would draw Japanese planes. The obvious choice for repairs was Australia, but Captain Robinson knew his ship could not withstand the relatively rough seas he would have to cross to get there, so he set course for Trincomalee, Ceylon, 4,000 miles across the Indian Ocean. Disappointment greeted *Marblehead* again at Ceylon as no suitable dock existed there either. However, the crew was pleased that the ship had not broken up, that the engines had not burned up, and that the Japanese had not found them on the voyage. Still in danger, the cruiser set out again and arrived safely in South Africa where she entered drydock and was

finally able to drain some 34 compartments. Repairs in South Africa allowed the ship to complete her journey to New York where she arrived on 4 May 1942. After a voyage of over 9,000 precarious miles, the cruiser entered drydock to be rebuilt. On 15 October 1942 she again put to sea.

The adventurous escape from the Java Sea was indeed miraculous and the heroism and seamanship exhibited between February and May 1942 rank as the major highlight in *Marblehead*'s career, but the cruiser continued to serve until the end of the war. Until February 1944 the cruiser operated in the South Atlantic, then steamed along the convoy routes of the North Atlantic until July 1944. In July 1944 *Marblehead* joined the task force preparing to invade southern France and in August she bombarded enemy installations near Saint Raphael. After conducting midshipmen cruises in 1945 the famed old cruiser was decommissioned 1 November 1945 and was sold for scrap 27 February 1946.

THE U.S.S. MARBLEHEAD COMES HOME!

Whenever men gather to speak of heroic deeds the saga of the Marblehead will rank with the greatest. After the battle of Macassar Strait this gallant ship took her place in the line and accepted the challenge of a vastly superior foe. With guns blazing a torrent of steel she fought her way clear only to be bombed without quarter from the skies.

The enemy reported her as sunk. With steering gear shattered, with great gaping holes in her sides, she

started her epic thirteen thousand mile voyage to safety. Only the courage, stamina and resourcefulness of men who would not "give up the ship" brought her home.

If good red fighting blood flows in your veins; if you want the comradeship of men such as those on the Marblehead--go to your nearest Navy Recruiting Station today!

There's a billet in the U. S. Navy waiting for you.

Wartime recruiting poster relating the saga of *Marblehead*. USN

The ship safe in New York, work begins to repair *Marblehead*'s damage, including a bent bow. NA

Damage to the fantail of *Marblehead* is evident in this picture taken at Tjilatjap, Java, where the cruiser stopped briefly for temporary repairs after the February 1942 Battle of the Java Sea. NA

THE BROOKLYN CLASS

ON 16 JUNE 1933 PRESIDENT ROOSEVELT ANNOUNCED that $238 million of the funds provided by the National Industrial Recovery Act would be allocated to increase contracts for the depressed shipbuilding industry and thereby help the U.S. Navy to build up to the strength allowed by the 1930 London Treaty. Having reached the treaty limit for heavy cruisers with its plans to build *Wichita* (CA-45), the Navy chose to build large 10,000-ton cruisers with fifteen 6-inch guns. Reasons for this decision centered on a response to the recent Japanese *Mogami*-class design; American naval officials wanted a long-ranging, rapid-firing, 6-inch gunned cruiser that could smother the slower-firing, 8-inch gunned cruisers.

The first four ships of this class (*Brooklyn* (CL-40), *Philadelphia* (CL-41), *Savannah* (CL-42) and *Nashville* (CL-43) were authorized in 1933 along with the soon-to-be-famous carriers *Yorktown* (CV-5) and *Enterprise* (CV-6). The remaining three cruisers (*Phoenix* (CL-46), *Boise* (CL-47) and *Honolulu* (CL-48) were funded by the 1934 Vinson-Trammell Act. As a class, these seven ships would fight throughout the war and would be found in both the Atlantic and Pacific. Together they would earn 49 battle stars (*Brooklyn* 4, *Philadelphia* 5, *Savannah* 3, *Nashville* 10, *Phoenix* 9, *Boise* 10 and *Honolulu* 8) and although several of these cruisers were damaged by enemy action, none was lost in World War II. The ships were decommissioned at war's end, but general consensus was that the combat performance of the class had been quite satisfactory.

About the only attribute shared by the *Brooklyn* class and the earlier *Omaha* class was their classification as light cruisers. Although still under treaty restrictions, the design of the *Brooklyns* was successful to the degree that it was not greatly altered in the design of the later *Helena* class and *Cleveland* class. Costing approximately $18.5 million each, the *Brooklyns* introduced the new flush-deck hull. They carried a peacetime complement of 868 officers and men, while the wartime complement rose to 1,200.

Overall length of the *Brooklyns* was 608 feet. For most of the class the beam measured 62 feet but *Philadelphia*, *Savannah* and *Honolulu* were modified and their beams measured 70 feet. Standard displacement ranged from 9,475 to 9,700 tons while average war service tonnage approached 13,000 tons. Draft was 25 feet maximum and the class was designed to reach a speed of 33 knots. Horsepower was 100,788; each ship had four screws and carried 2,175 tons of oil which provided a cruising radius of 3,800 miles at 25 knots or 7,800 miles at 15 knots.

Protection for the *Brooklyns* went well beyond the small water-line section of the 3-inch armor on the *Omahas*. Whereas the armor patch on the *Omahas* covered one-third of their length, the 1.5-inch to 5-inch side armor of the *Brooklyns* covered approximately 70 percent. Further, deck armor was 2.5 plus 3 inches, turrets had 3 inches to 5 inches of protection and the conning tower was 8 inches thick.

Main armament for the *Brooklyns* consisted of fifteen 6-inch guns arranged in five triple turrets. Three turrets were forward and two aft with turrets number two and four in super-firing (raised) positions. This pattern was not unique as the Japanese *Takao* class cruisers had the same disposition and the British *Nelson*-class battleships had the same pattern forward. However, the design was not entirely successful—the number three turret had a limited arc of training. Still, these ships could provide an excellent broadside. Secondary armament included eight 5-inch guns (single mounts on all but *Savannah* and *Honolulu* which had their 5-inch, dual-purpose batteries in enclosed twin mounts). Like other prewar combatants, the original 1.1-inch quads were replaced by the later 40mm Bofors (18 to 28 barrels) and the .50-caliber machine guns were replaced by 20mm Oerlikons (14 to 28).

New to all American warships was the design of a high, square stern which contained a built-in fantail hangar. The two catapults aft were served by a single crane. Although this design was incorporated into the later *Helena*-class and *Cleveland*-class light cruisers as well as the *Wichita*- and *Baltimore*-class heavy cruisers, there were problems: the hangar was directly over the shafts and propellers which caused vibration, and recovering float planes was more difficult over the stern than amidships due to the greater vertical movement of the ship at the stern. Too, there was concern for possible flooding in the hangar area. The ships were designed to carry as many as six planes in the hangar, but usually no more than four were carried during operations.

At the end of World War II all members of the class were quickly decommissioned but five were later sold to South American countries. One of these, *Phoenix*—a survivor of Pearl Harbor—would once again experience the horror of war.

BROOKLYN CL-40

(4 Battle Stars) Named for a borough in New York City, *Brooklyn* (CL-40) was laid down 12 March 1935 at the New York Navy Yard. The class leader was sponsored at her launch on 30 November 1936 by Miss Kathryn Jane Lackey and was commissioned 30 September 1937 with Capt. W.D. Brereton Jr. commanding.

Highlights of *Brooklyn*'s prewar career centered on helping to open the New York World's Fair in April 1939 and acting as base ship during the salvage and rescue operations of the sunken submarine *Squalus* in May 1939 (SS-192 sank on trials but 33 of 59 crew members were rescued, and the sub was raised and served under the new name *Sailfish*.) The cruiser also participated in the opening of the Golden Gate Exposition in February 1940. Destined to spend her entire wartime career in the Atlantic, the cruiser served with the Pacific Fleet from late 1939 until May 1941. In July 1941 *Brooklyn* assumed duties as a convoy escort in the North Atlantic and as a unit of the Neutrality Patrol.

Early wartime duty was spent patrolling in the Caribbean, but in April 1942 she was back in the North Atlantic as a convoy escort between the United States and the United Kingdom. On 3 September the cruiser took aboard 1,173 troops from *Wakefield* (AP-21) which had caught fire and had to be abandoned. On 8 November *Brooklyn* bombarded shore installations during "Operation Torch" off North Africa. Hit by a dud enemy shell, the cruiser suffered damage to two guns and counted five men wounded. Before engaging in combat again the cruiser escorted three convoys from the United States to Casablanca. In July 1943 *Brooklyn* provided fire support during the invasions of Sicily and then covered the Anzio landing January-February 1944. On 15 August 1944 she furnished gunfire which preceded Allied landings in southern France and she remained in the Mediterranean until November. From December 1944 until the end of the European war in May 1945 the cruiser underwent repairs at the same yard where she had been built. She was not ordered to the Pacific for the remaining three months of that conflict, and the cruiser went into reserve 30 January 1946 and was decommissioned 3 January 1947. On 9 January 1951 *Brooklyn* was transferred to the navy of Chile where she was renamed *O'Higgins*. There she served until running aground in 1974 after which she was used as an accommodation ship. Modernized in the late 1970s, the ship was still operational into 1983.

The last surviving combat-active World War II cruiser, *Brooklyn* is seen here off New York City in 1939. Today, she is still serving the navy of Chile as *O'Higgins*. USN

Port-side view of *Brooklyn*, circa 1938. Note arrangement of main armament and compare overall configuration, minus armament, to that of *Wichita*. USN

PHILADELPHIA CL-41

(5 Battle Stars, Navy Unit Commendation) Named for the city in eastern Pennsylvania, *Philadelphia* (CL-41) was laid down 28 May 1935 at the Philadelphia Navy Yard. The cruiser was sponsored by Mrs. George H. Earle on 17 November 1936 at the launch and was placed in commission 23 September 1937 with Capt. Jules James in command.

The operational history of *Philadelphia* was quite similar to that of *Brooklyn*. In the Pacific for only a relatively short prewar period (June 1939-June 1941), the *Philadelphia* participated in the Neutrality Patrol and was undergoing maintenance in Boston when war was declared. Anti-submarine patrol in eastern Atlantic waters was interspersed with convoy duty in the North Atlantic until the cruiser was assigned to the November 1942 North African operation. *Philadelphia* dueled enemy shore batteries and her spotter planes bombed and damaged at least one Vichy French submarine. Following more convoy duty that lasted into the spring of 1943, the cruiser operated off Sicily in July and August and particularly distinguished herself in the action around Palermo by accurate gunfire against German tanks and by helping to fight off several air attacks. In February 1944 *Philadelphia* provided shore bombardment near Anzio and continued on station into May. In the late summer and early fall of 1944 the cruiser participated in the invasion of southern France and then reported to her namesake city for overhaul, never to return to combat.

In July 1945 *Philadelphia* escorted *Augusta* (CA-31) when the latter ship carried President Harry Truman to Antwerp en route to the Potsdam Conference. After the return trip in August, the cruiser enjoyed the fruits of victory by celebrating Navy Day in her namesake city and joining the "Magic Carpet" fleet. Inactivated 9 January 1946, the cruiser was decommissioned 3 February 1947. On 9 January 1951 she was sold to Brazil and renamed *Barroso*. The old American cruiser served in the Brazilian Navy until stricken in 1973.

Philadelphia (foreground) with *Pensacola* and *Salt Lake City*, circa 1938.   NA

SAVANNAH CL-42

(3 Battle Stars) Named for the coastal city in Georgia, *Savannah* (CL-42) was laid down 31 May 1934 by the New York Shipbuilding Corp. The ship was sponsored at her launch on 8 May 1937 by Jayne M. Bowden and was commissioned 10 March 1938. Capt. Robert C. Griffen was *Savannah*'s first commander.

Like her two sister ships, *Brooklyn* and *Philadelphia*, *Savannah* trained in the Pacific for nearly two years and then operated exclusively in the European theater during the war. After prewar Neutrality Patrol duty and convoy escort, the cruiser began her wartime experience patrolling the Caribbean with carrier *Ranger* (CV-4). A major function of the Caribbean patrol was to keep watch on Vichy French warships at Martinique and Guadaloupe. With *Brooklyn* and *Philadelphia*, *Savannah* helped cover the November 1942 invasion of North Africa.

In January 1943 *Savannah* teamed with escort carrier *Santee* and destroyers to patrol the South Atlantic for German blockade runners. In March *Savannah* and destroyer *Eberle* intercepted an enemy ship whose crew promptly set explosive charges to scuttle their vessel. *Savannah* took aboard 72 prisoners. She then returned to New York for overhaul and preparation for assignment to the Mediterranean. Off Sicily in July 1943 the cruiser provided gunfire support, but had three of her four spotter planes shot down early in the battle.

Continuing her gunfire support, the cruiser took aboard wounded American infantrymen for medical aid and also fought enemy planes. On the night of 8 September 1943, *Savannah* entered Salerno Bay in Italy to bombard enemy positions, and she continued close support until the morning of 11 September when the ship was hit and damaged by a radio-controlled glide bomb released from a German plane. The bomb passed through the number three turret roof and three decks before exploding. The blast blew a large hole in the bottom of the ship and opened a seam on the port side as well as starting serious fires. Killed were 197 men—nearly one-fifth of the crew. After emergency repairs at Malta, the cruiser steamed to Philadelphia where she was under repair until September 1944.

Savannah never returned to combat but did escort *Quincy* (CA-71) which was carrying President Roosevelt toward the Yalta Conference in February 1945. After the return voyage the cruiser served as a school ship for nucleus crews of ships that were not ready for commissioning, and as a training ship for midshipmen. After enjoying the late-October 1945 Navy Day celebrations in her namesake city, the cruiser sailed as part of the "Magic Carpet" fleet. Inactivated 22 April 1946, the ship was decommissioned 3 February 1947. She was sold for scrap 25 January 1966.

Savannah on a full-power run off Maine in February 1938.   USN

After nearly 40 years, Navy veterans of World War II can still recall exact scores and details of athletic contests between ships. Here, *Savannah's* basketball team is shown in 1938. After a hiatus in 1942, athletic competition resumed on a limited scale between ships' teams. USN

Crewmen fight fires resulting from a German radio-controlled glide bomb. The bomb hit *Savannah's* number three turret, passed through three decks, blew holes in the bottom and side of the cruiser and killed 197 men. Note wounded and dead on deck. NA

NASHVILLE CL-43

(10 Battle Stars) A busy and effective ship from the beginning of World War II until its conclusion, *Nashville* (CL-43)—named for the capital city of Tennessee—was laid down 24 January 1935 by the New York Shipbuilding Corp. The cruiser was sponsored at her launch by Miss Ann Stahlman and Miss Mildred Stahlman on 2 October 1937 and was commissioned 6 June 1938 with Capt. William W. Wilson in command.

Nashville, with her earlier sister ships, operated in the Pacific during most of the final two years before America's entry into war. Detached from the Pacific in May 1941, the cruiser was based in the Caribbean when Pearl Harbor was attacked. With the advent of war *Nashville* escorted a convoy to Iceland and operated in the Atlantic until 4 March 1942 when she joined carrier *Hornet* (CV-8) off Virginia and escorted the carrier all the way to the shores of Japan for the 18 April Halsey-Doolittle Tokyo raid. The accompanying destroyers were detached in the final days of the mission and only *Nashville* along with the other escorting cruisers and the two carriers—B-25 loaded *Hornet* and Halsey's flagship *Enterprise*— closed for the surprise launch. Discovered by Japanese patrol craft before reaching the desired launching point, the B-25s were flown off early. *Nashville*'s crew was frustrated when it was not able to destroy one of the pickets before that boat could radio the news of the intruders. Despite the difficulty of get-

ting off accurate salvos at a small target in rough seas, *Nashville*'s gunners claimed two patrol vessels for the famous "Shangri-La" force.

The cruiser next moved to Alaska in May 1942 and participated in the Kiska attack, staying in the Aleutians until November 1942. *Nashville* then steamed to the Solomons, where six American cruisers had already been sunk by the time she arrived in December 1942. The cruiser escorted troopships to Guadalcanal and joined *Helena* and *St. Louis* in bombarding an enemy air base at Munda on the evening of 4 January 1943. Joining additional attacks in the region throughout the winter and spring of 1943, the cruiser suffered only one bad experience: on 12 May 1943 an explosion of powder charges in a forward turret killed 18 and wounded 17.

After repairs and modernization at San Francisco, *Nashville* returned to take part in raids against Marcus Island and Wake Island in the fall of 1943 and then moved again into the southwest Pacific where she attacked targets in New Guinea and the Admiralty Islands. Names such as Bougainville, Cape Gloucester and Hollandia became known to the veterans of *Nashville* as they saw their ship's guns alter the landscape of these enemy-held locations. She served as a constant seaborne command post for Gen. Douglas MacArthur and his staff during the succession of invasions in the region, and *Nashville* also carried the general on his promised return

Army B-25s warm up on *Hornet's* flight deck as *Nashville* provides escort for the 18 April 1942 Halsey-Doolittle Tokyo raid.
USN

to the Philippines in October 1944. After safely depositing her famous guest, the cruiser returned to her role as fire-support ship and air-defense platform. While off the Philippines on 13 December 1944 the cruiser was hit by a kamikaze on her port side. Resulting explosions and fire killed 133, wounded 190, and inflicted damage topside. Repaired by mid-March 1945, the cruiser returned to the war in the late spring and supported the landings at Brunei Bay, Borneo. She was at sea seeking an enemy convoy off Indochina when the war ended. *Nashville* then transported troops to the West Coast before being decommissioned 24 June 1946. Sold to Chile 9 January 1951, the cruiser was renamed *Captain Prat*, later *Chacabuco*, and she was still active into 1982.

Nashville bombards Kiska in the Aleutians 8 August 1942.

USN

PHOENIX CL-46

(9 Battle Stars) Blessed with good luck for 99 percent of her 44-year life, *Phoenix* (CL-46), named for the capital city of Arizona, was laid down 15 April 1935 by the New York Shipbuilding Corp. Sponsored at the launch on 13 March 1938 by Mrs. Dorothea Kays Moonan, the cruiser was commissioned 3 October 1938 and steamed on her shakedown cruise with Capt. John W. Rankin in command. Ironically, her shakedown cruise itinerary included Argentina, her future and final home.

Phoenix was assigned to the Pacific when ready for duty, and was in Pearl Harbor during the 7 December 1941 attack. A robust anti-aircraft fire from her guns helped *Phoenix* to provide one of the few bright spots for the U.S. Navy; she finished the day's battle with only a single bullet hole inflicted upon her. The cruiser's schedule for the first months of war was consumed by convoy duty between Hawaii and the West Coast of the United States along with a run to Australia. After a stint in the Indian Ocean and waters around Australia in late 1942 and early 1943, *Phoenix* was overhauled in July 1943. Before returning to the Pacific she carried Secretary of State Cordell Hull to Casablanca.

In December 1943 and the early months of 1944 *Phoenix* operated in the southwest Pacific supporting invasion forces. Often in company with sister ship *Nashville*, *Phoenix* was constantly in combat throughout the remainder of 1944. After the fighting around New Guinea, *Phoenix* moved with MacArthur to the Philippines and there fought in the Battle of Surigao Strait, which brought an end to surface battles between capital ships. She remained on station off the Philippines and in southwestern Pacific waters until the last month of the war, and the cruiser fought innumerable kamikazes and provided covering gunfire in support of landings. En route to Pearl Harbor for a long-overdue overhaul when the war concluded, *Phoenix* continued on to the Atlantic. Placed in reserve 28 February 1946, the cruiser was decommissioned 3 July 1946. She was transferred to Argentina 9 April 1951 and was renamed *17 de Octubre* but renamed *General Belgrano* in 1956.

After the heavy cruiser *St. Paul* (CA-73) was scrapped in 1980, the *Phoenix-General Belgrano* was the last of two all-gun World War II cruisers that had served in the U.S. Navy. As no World War II cruiser had been memorialized, cruiser survivor groups turned their attention to Argentina in hope of acquiring the old cruiser as a floating museum. Still greatly resembling her World War II appearance, she would have been a major attraction to World War II Navy veterans and historians. However, luck finally deserted the 44-year-old cruiser on 2 May 1982 when a British submarine hit her with two torpedoes. The ship went down in 15 minutes and took 321 Argentine sailors with her. The Falklands War was a tragedy for historic friends Britain and Argentina and it was a great loss for naval history.

Starboard view of *Phoenix* in 1938 soon after commissioning. On 2 May 1982 this cruiser, serving in the navy of Argentina as *General Belgrano*, was sunk by two torpedoes fired by a British submarine. USN

Phoenix passing the burning *Arizona* during the attack on Pearl Harbor 7 December 1941. Despite all the mayhem of battle on that day, *Phoenix* suffered only one bullet hole, thereby giving much more than she received. USN

BOISE CL-47

(10 Battle Stars) Named for the capital of Idaho, *Boise* (CL-47) was laid down 1 April 1935 by the Newport News Shipbuilding and Dry Dock Co. The cruiser was sponsored at her launch 3 December 1936 by Miss Salome Clark, daughter of the governor of Idaho, and the ship was commissioned 12 August 1938 with Capt. B.U. McCandlish in command.

Boise spent most of the short period between commissioning and war operating in the Pacific, and she was off the Philippines when war broke. She was most always a ship of good fortune. She struck an uncharted shoal on 21 January 1942 and had to make her way back to San Francisco for repairs; had this event not occurred she might well have been lost in the February Battle of the Java Sea which claimed *Houston* (CA-30) and other Allied warships. Assigned to the Solomons Campaign in the late summer of 1942, she fulfilled several assignments off Guadalcanal before engaging in the 11-12 October 1942 Battle of Cape Esperance (see *Salt Lake City* for details of battle). In this battle, which was an American tactical victory and strategic draw, *Boise* recorded numerous hits on the Japanese cruisers and destroyers, but she too became a target when she turned on a searchlight to illuminate her prey. At least six enemy shells hit *Boise*. One demolished the interior of turret number one. Another hit detonated a magazine, and for a few moments it appeared the entire ship would be blasted to bits. However, other hits opened the hull and water flooded the forward magazines. With 107 dead, 35 wounded and the forward section of the cruiser at once burning and flooding, *Boise* limped away from the action. Returning to the Philadelphia Navy Yard for repairs, she was hailed by the press as the "one-ship task force." Although *Boise* was worthy of praise, the attention caused resentment aboard other ships that had fought off Cape Esperance and could not be identified due to wartime censorship.

After repairs *Boise* steamed to the Mediterranean. In July-August 1943 she helped cover landings on Sicily and in September she participated in the landings on the Italian penninsula. Assigned once again to the South Pacific, she arrived there at the end of the year and spent all of

Boise fitting out at Newport News in 1938. The carriers fitting out are *Enterprise* (left) and *Yorktown*.   NA

1944 and the early months of 1945 fighting along the coast of New Guinea and through the Philippines. Throughout this period she was often in company with sister ships *Nashville* and *Phoenix*. After *Nashville* was damaged, *Boise* embarked General MacArthur twice, once for the Lingayen Gulf landings and from 3-16 June 1945 she carried the future ruler of occupied Japan on a 3,500-mile tour of the recaptured Philippine Islands.

After participating in the gigantic 27 October 1945 Navy Day celebration at New York City, the ship remained there until decommissioned 1 July 1946. She was sold to Argentina 11 January 1951 and was renamed *Nueve de Julio*. She served until 1979 when she was stricken.

A crewmember examines damage to *Boise* after the October 1942 Battle of Cape Esperance. Badly damaged and with 107 dead, the cruiser was fortunate to survive the battle.   NA

Night view of *Boise* bombarding Sicily in July 1943. *Boise* was one of only a few cruisers to see combat against both Germany and Japan.   NA

Receiving the laurels of victory, *Boise* rides at anchor during the October 1945 Navy Day celebration in New York City.

USN

HONOLULU CL-48

(8 Battle Stars, Navy Unit Commendation) A participant in several of the Pacific war's more notable battles, *Honolulu* (CL-48) was named for the capital city of Hawaii. Laid down at the New York Navy Yard on 10 September 1935, the cruiser was sponsored at her launch on 26 August 1937 by Miss Helen Poindexter, daughter of Hawaii's governor. *Honolulu* was commissioned 15 June 1938 with Capt. Oscar Smith in command.

Reporting to the Pacific in June 1939, *Honolulu* trained off the West Coast of the United States and Hawaii in the prewar years. The ship was in Pearl Harbor on the day of the Japanese surprise attack. Slightly damaged by a near miss, she was quickly repaired and began convoy duty as the military acted to reinforce Pacific bases. Responding to the Japanese Alaskan feint during the Battle of Midway, *Honolulu* and other ships were ordered north. In August 1942 *Honolulu* took part in the bombardment of Kiska and screened the initial American landings in the Aleutians at Adak. Reassigned soon after, *Honolulu* steamed to the Solomons where on 30 November-1 December 1942 she fought in the disastrous Battle of Tassafaronga (see *Northampton* for details), in which *Northampton* was lost and *New Orleans*, *Minneapolis* and *Pensacola* were severely damaged. In 1983 some survivors of the lost and damaged cruisers still harbor ill feelings toward *Honolulu* as she did not stop to

pick them out of the water. However, *Honolulu* was still under fire—some of it from American ships—and was under orders to search for and pursue the enemy. However, the admiral aboard *Honolulu* did order two destroyers to rescue the cruiser sailors in the water.

By July 1943 *Honolulu* had fought her way up the Solomons chain and had gained a reputation as a fighting ship that the enemy could not touch. But the law of averages was about to apply to the veteran combatant. After emerging from the 6 July 1943 Battle of Kula Gulf (see *Helena* for details) in which two enemy destroyers were lost along with cruiser *Helena*, *Honolulu* moved on the evening of 13 July to intercept a large enemy destroyer-transport force carrying troops and supplies from Rabaul to Vila. Led by a single light cruiser, *Jintsu*, the Japanese force was met by *Honolulu*, *St. Louis* (CL-49), the old Australian cruiser *Leander* and 10 destroyers. At the conclusion of the Battle of Kolombangara, the combat-proven *Jintsu* had been sunk—thanks in part to the shelling received from *Honolulu*—but the American destroyer *Gwin* had been lost and all three Allied cruisers had taken torpedoes. *Honolulu* was hit twice, once by a dud in the stern which did little damage, and once forward of turret number one. The bow of *Honolulu* collapsed much like that of *Minneapolis* at Tassafaronga. Incredibly there were no casualties, but

Honolulu shows the effect of a Japanese destroyer-launched torpedo just after the 13 July 1943 Battle of Kolombangara. Incredibly, no lives were lost.   USN

No stranger to repair facilities, *Honolulu* is shown here in drydock to repair damage inflicted by an aerial torpedo, 20 October 1944. Sixty men were lost.   USN

the cruiser was out of the war for four months.

Before the end of the year *Honolulu* was back in the South Pacific to again bring pain to the enemy. From action off Bougainville, the cruiser moved with portions of the fleet in 1944 to Saipan, Guam, Peleliu, and finally to the Philippines. The fleet would move on toward Japan after the Philippine Campaign, but on 20 October 1944 *Honolulu* was hit by an aerial torpedo on her port side under turret number three. Sixty officers and men were killed—the cruiser's first casualties after nearly three years of continuous battles. Before the wounded cruiser could move away from the area, she was hit by "friendly" gunfire and five more were killed.

Long overdue for overhaul and now in need of repair, *Honolulu* spent the remainder of the war at Norfork, Va. Repaired, she served as a training ship in the fall of 1945 and was decommissioned 3 February 1947. On 17 November 1949 the much-traveled cruiser was sold for scrap.

THE HELENA CLASS

IN NEARLY ALL ESSENTIAL CHARACTERISTICS THE two-ship *Helena* class was similar to the *Brooklyn* class. Many naval histories do not separate the *Helenas* and *Brooklyns* and instead state that the *Brooklyn* class had nine units, including *Helena* (CL-50) and *St. Louis* (CL-49). Due to the close similarity in dimensions, propulsion, armament, protection, and overall appearance, this introduction to the *Helena* class will record only the differences between the *Helenas* and *Brooklyns*.

The most obvious difference distinguishing the *Helenas* from the *Brooklyns* was the placement of the after superstructure immediately behind the number two stack. Minor differences included the *Helenas'* placement of the mainmast just aft of the number two stack and the placement of enclosed twin 5-inch gun mounts. The 5-inch gun mounts of the *Helenas* were similar to the design of *Savannah* and *Honolulu*, which were both different from the other five *Brooklyns*.

Authorized in 1935 from the same legislation that authorized the *Brooklyns*, the *Helena* and *St. Louis* were outstanding fighting ships. *St. Louis* earned 11 battle stars and *Helena* won 7 while becoming the first ship to earn the Navy Unit Commendation. Before she was sunk in July 1943, *Helena* earned a well-deserved reputation as an effective, courageous fighter. Had she survived the war her fame would have made her a candidate for preservation, but given the disappointing record regarding the preservation of World War II's most famous ships, *Helena* too probably would have been scrapped.

HELENA CL-50

(**7 Battle Stars, Navy Unit Commendation**) Primarily remembered for her valor in battle, *Helena* (CL-50), named for the capital of Montana, was laid down 9 December 1936 at the New York Navy Yard. Sponsored at her launch 27 August 1939 by Miss E.C. Gudger, a granddaughter of Montana's Sen. Thomas J. Welch, the cruiser was commissioned 18 September 1939 with Capt. Max B. Demott in command.

She was in the berth normally occupied by Pacific Fleet flagship *Pennsylvania* when the Japanese arrived on Sunday morning 7 December 1941. A single aerial torpedo passed under minelayer *Oglala*, which was moored alongside, and hit *Helena* amidships on her starboard side. Watertight integrity was quickly achieved by the ship's crew, and her enthusiastic anti-aircraft fire discouraged enemy airmen from attacking the cruiser again at close range. Partially repaired at Pearl, *Helena* steamed to San Francisco for permanent repair and overhaul.

Off Guadalcanal on 15 September 1942 *Helena*'s crew helped rescue survivors of carrier *Wasp* which was sunk by submarine torpedoes. Four weeks later the cruiser exacted vengeance for earlier wounds by pouring 6-inch shells into cruiser *Furutaka* and destroyer *Fubuki* (both were sunk in this action) and other enemy warships in the 11-12 October 1942 Battle of Cape Esperance (see *Salt Lake City* for details of battle). And four weeks after Cape Esperance, *Helena* was one of 13 American warships that fought in the 13 November Naval Battle of Guadalcanal. She was one of four that was still operational the following day.

In the early months of 1943 the cruiser was primarily occupied with shore bombardments in the New Georgia area. On 5 July 1943 she began her last operation by escorting transports to landings on New Georgia and by providing covering fire. Challenged by the enemy on the night of 6 July in what history remembers as the Battle of Kula Gulf, *Helena* turned her guns toward the 10 Japanese destroyers. Of the three cruisers and four destroyers in the American force, *Helena* became the favored target of aim for Japanese torpedoes because she lacked flashless powder. *Honolulu* and *St. Louis* did have flashless powder for their first salvos and the American

One of the great fighting ships of all time, *Helena* is seen here early in the war. Note 5-inch gun mounts, a distinguishing feature from most of the *Brooklyns*.   USN

Close-up of the aft section of *Helena*, June 1941. Note catapults and built-in hangar at stern.   USN

destroyers initially held fire trying to set up a torpedo launch. Believed by the Japanese to be firing 6-inch machine guns, *Helena* blazed away and contributed to the sinking of enemy destroyer *Niizuki* before the first of three Japanese torpedoes exploded against her hull.

The first torpedo hit below number one turret and sheared off the bow of the cruiser. The next two torpedoes hit under the second stack. In only a few minutes the cruiser jackknifed and sank. Most of the cruiser's survivors were picked up before morning, but many were not saved until some 11 days later. Some of those not rescued on the 6th clustered around the slowly sinking bow, made land and were rescued the following day. A

larger group—considerably aided by lifeboats and life-jackets dropped from a Navy plane and by two coast-watchers and natives of Vella Lavella—was picked up by destroyers on 17 July after several harrowing days in the water and on the enemy-held island. One hundred sixty-eight men of the great ship did not survive the battle or the abandonment. Many of the survivors, like those of cruisers lost earlier, were reassigned to new cruisers (over 400 of *Helena's* crew went to the new *Houston* (CL-81) and battleships—*Helena's* fighting spirit lived on. Of the 10 American cruisers lost in World War II, *Helena* was the last until *Indianapolis* was lost only days before the end of the war.

Already torpedoed, *Helena* (center) rides on an even keel during the Pearl Harbor attack 7 December 1941. Quick and effective damage control prevented *Helena* from suffering the fate of the capsized *Oglala* which is immediately behind the cruiser.   NA

ST. LOUIS CL-49

(11 Battle Stars, Navy Unit Commendation) Named for the riverfront city in Missouri, *St. Louis* (CL-49) was laid down 10 December 1936 at the Newport News Shipbuilding and Dry Dock Co. Sponsored at her launch on 15 April 1938 by Miss Nancy Lee Merrill, the cruiser was commissioned 19 May 1939 with Capt. Charles H. Morrison commanding.

After nearly a year of Neutrality Patrol operations, *St. Louis* transferred to the Pacific, arriving at Pearl Harbor 12 December 1940. She was in the harbor during the Japanese attack almost a year later, and the cruiser helped down three enemy planes and managed to leave the harbor before the battle was over. Her first months of war focused on convoy duty for troops and escort duty for carrier *Yorktown*(CV-5) during the February 1942 Marshalls-Gilberts raids. After further convoy duty the cruiser moved to the Aleutians for the summer months of 1942 where she conducted patrols, shelled Kiska and covered the occupation of Adak.

By January 1943 *St. Louis* was in the Solomons where her major missions were to stop enemy reinforcement landings and provide bombardment of enemy positions. On 6 July 1943 the cruiser fought in the Battle of Kula Gulf (see *Helena*) in which her only sister ship, *Helena*, was lost along with two enemy destroyers. Less than a week later, on 13 July, *St. Louis* joined with *Honolulu* and New Zealand light cruiser *Leander* and 10 destroyers to sink enemy light cruiser *Jintsu* in the Battle of Kolombangara. In this battle the American destroyer *Gwin* was lost, while *Leander* and *Honolulu* were damaged and *St. Louis* lost a chunk of her bow to a Japanese torpedo. Under repair for three months, *St. Louis* was back in the Solomons in November 1943. After covering Marine landings on Bougainville that month, the cruiser continued combat operations in the region until damaged by an aerial bomb on 14 February 1944 that killed 23 and wounded 20. Back in action by the following month, *St. Louis* resumed operations in the Solomons before moving on to the Marianas campaign in June 1944. Despite damage to one of her four shafts, the cruiser completed her assignments off Guam in July.

Overhauled in the late summer of 1944, *St. Louis* steamed to the Philippines in November 1944, but soon after arrival she was attacked by Japanese planes and damaged again. A burning suicide plane struck the ship and before all fires were out from this attack a second burning enemy plane crashed on the cruiser. Sixteen men were killed in these two crashes and 43 were wounded. Repaired once more at San Francisco the veteran cruiser returned to the fleet and screened carriers as they made their final raids on the Japanese home islands.

Occupation duties in the Far East were followed by several "Magic Carpet" runs. Decommissioned 20 June 1946, the fighting cruiser was sold to Brazil in January 1951. She served that country as *Tamadare* until stricken in 1975.

Port-side view of *St. Louis* in November 1942.   USN

Despite victory in the 13 July 1943 Battle of Kolombangara, *St. Louis* lost a significant portion of her bow to an enemy destroyer-launched torpedo. Another ship behind the cruiser partially obscures the extent of damage.

USN

THE ATLANTA-OAKLAND CLASS

UNIQUE AMONG CRUISERS OF THE UNITED STATES Navy during World War II, the *Atlanta-Oakland*-class cruisers were designed to function as flotilla leaders in anticipation of fighting high-speed Japanese destroyers. Inspired by the design of the British *Dido*-class anti-aircraft cruisers, the *Atlantas* were also to serve as high-speed, rapid-shooting, anti-aircraft gun platforms.

Altogether 11 ships of this class were authorized and laid down. However, only eight fought and earned battle stars. The eight battle-star-winning cruisers were *Atlanta* (CL-51) with 5, *Juneau* (CL-52) with 4, *San Diego* (CL-53) with 15, *San Juan* (CL-54) with 13, *Oakland* (CL-95) with 9, *Reno* (CL-96) with 3, *Flint* (CL-97) with 4 and *Tucson* (CL-98) with 1. As a class these ships totaled 54 battle stars and *Atlanta* was awarded the Presidential Unit Citation.

Authorization for the *Atlanta* class stemmed from the Vinson-Trammel Act of 1934. At that time authorization was for the U.S. Navy to be provided with funds to build cruisers up to treaty strength. The design of the *Atlanta-Oakland* class had not been accepted in 1934 and the first four ships were not planned for construction until the 1939 program. The first four *Oaklands*, and the last of this class to serve in combat, were included in the 1940 program.

Costing over $23 million each, the *Atlantas* carried a complement of 600 to 800 officers and men. Overall length was 541 feet, shorter than all other American World War II light cruisers including the *Omahas*. Beam measurement was 53 feet (54 feet for the *Oaklands*), draft ranged from 21 to 27 feet and displacement was 6,000 tons standard and 8,200 tons when loaded for combat. Therefore, in all aspects of size the *Atlantas* were considerably smaller than all other U.S. Navy light cruisers of the era.

Designed to achieve 38 knots, the *Atlantas* were too overloaded to achieve the desired speed that would allow them to run with high-speed destroyers. Under combat conditions best speed was 32-33 knots. Horsepower was 75,000, each vessel had two screws (they were the only American light cruiser class with two; all others had four), and each had a capacity for 1,528 tons of oil which provided a cruising radius of 4,000 miles at 25 knots or 7,700 miles at 15 knots.

By no standard could the *Atlantas* be considered well protected. Indeed, the only two members of the class to engage in a major surface battle were sunk. Side armor ranged up to 3.5 inches with deck armor measuring 2 inches. There was very little protection in the superstructure for either guns (1.25-inch turrets) or for the bridge (some later units had bridge armor installed) as topside weight was a known problem even in the design stage. One early recognition of the topside weight problem was the deletion of catapults and float planes thereby making the *Atlantas* the only cruiser class not to be so equipped.

Although unique in several characteristics, armament was the most significant distinguishing feature of the *Atlantas* as this was the only cruiser class to carry dual-purpose 5-inch guns as the ships' main battery. Too, slight changes in armament were the only noteworthy differences between the first four ships of the class (*Atlantas*) and the later members (*Oaklands*). The first four ships were armed with eight twin 5-inch turrets (5-inch guns are usually referred to as "mounts" but the term "turrets" is used here to signify main battery) for a total of 16 barrels. Six of the twin turrets were on the centerline, three forward and three aft, with the other two waist turrets abeam the after superstructure. The later *Oaklands* did not carry the two waist 5-inch turrets, but they did carry more of the intermediate-range 40mm Bofors which soon replaced the 1.1-inch guns. The *Oaklands* carried 16 to 24 40mm barrels while the *Atlantas* carried 10 to 14. Installation of 20mm guns was similar; the *Atlantas* mounted nine to 15 while the *Oaklands* had 16. Both carried two quad, above-water torpedo tubes. With their 5-inch guns, torpedo tubes and two depth charge tracks, the *Atlanta* class ships might have been better classified as super destroyers rather than light cruisers.

Historical views on the wartime success of these cruisers are mixed. The early ships experienced difficulty in their primary function of fighting enemy planes due to a lack of sufficient directors for the main battery. Also, more intermediate anti-aircraft guns were needed in 1942. As these problems were addressed in late 1942 and throughout the remainder of the war, trade-offs had to occur for the ships to maintain stability. Topweight was a pervasive problem throughout the lives of these cruisers.

The flush deck, forward sheer and superstructure arrangement of the *Atlantas* resembled the *Cleveland*-class light cruisers, but turret arrangement and the absence of a crane at the stern quickly distinguished one from the other. Finally, the concept of the small, fast, anti-aircraft cruiser is still alive in the contemporary U.S. Navy as missile-firing vessels continue the basic function of the *Atlantas* and often show similarities of design.

ATLANTA CL-51

(5 Battle Stars, Presidential Unit Citation) The only light cruiser to be awarded the Presidential Unit Citation in World War II, *Atlanta* (CL-51), named for the capital city of Georgia, was laid down 22 April 1940 by the Federal Shipbuilding and Dry Dock Co., Kearny, N.J. Sponsored by Margaret Mitchell, author of *Gone With The Wind*, the cruiser was launched 6 September 1941 and was commissioned only three months later on 24 December 1941. *Atlanta*'s first commanding officer, Capt. S.P. Jenkins, was to be the ship's only commanding officer.

War officially began two weeks before *Atlanta* joined the fleet and training was therefore expedited. During the crucial 4-6 June 1942 Battle of Midway *Atlanta* was in the screen for *Enterprise* and *Hornet*, but these ships did not come under attack. Two months later, however, *Atlanta* joined heavy cruiser *Portland* and battleship *North Carolina* in the screen for *Enterprise* during the 24 August 1942 Battle of the Eastern Solomons. In one of the war's two heaviest air attacks against an American carrier, *Atlanta* had ample opportunity to perform in her primary air defense role. Lessons learned from this battle had considerable expression in the modification of later cruisers of the class—i.e., more gun directors and more intermediate anti-aircraft guns.

In the early morning hours of 13 November 1942 *Atlanta* was in a line of 13 American cruisers and destroyers which ran headlong into a Japanese formation of 14 warships that included two battleships. The night action of 13 November was the first of three major battles over a three-day period (13-15 November), but *Atlanta* lived only to fight in the battle of the 13th. Being the first cruiser in the American formation, *Atlanta* drew initial attention from the enemy and beams of light illuminated her. *Atlanta*'s guns extinguished several enemy spotlights and blazed away at enemy ships on both sides of her. Within 10 minutes, however, the cruiser built to fight planes, destroyers and submarines had taken at least one torpedo and approximately 50 major-caliber hits including several from battleship *Hiei*. On fire, taking water, and without power, *Atlanta* drifted out of the fight, but before the confused battle ended the wounded cruiser took two more devastating broadsides from a cruiser. The last two salvos were believed to have been fired by *USS San Francisco*, which ironically was one of the other two American World War II cruisers to win the Presidential Unit Citation and which won the award for this same action.

At daylight the cruiser was still afloat and she remained afloat until dark when the decision was made to scuttle the ship. Beaching was out of the question due to the presence of the enemy and repair facilities were too far distant for the terribly hurt ship. One hundred seventy-two men died with their ship and 79 were wounded. Today the cruiser rests at the bottom of Savo Sound about three miles off Lunga Point, Guadalcanal.

Atlanta going down the ways 6 September 1941.   USN

Atlanta's sponsor, Margaret Mitchell, author of *Gone With The Wind,* at the launching ceremony, Kearny, N.J., 6 September 1941.   USN

Atlanta underway soon after being commissioned on Christmas Eve 1941, only 15 weeks after launching.   USN

During the June 1942 Battle of Midway, *Atlanta* steams past carrier *Hornet* to render assistance to a destroyer. Cruiser *New Orleans* is in the background.   NA

JUNEAU CL-52

(4 Battle Stars) One of the sadder and more tragic stories of the U.S. Navy in World War II is that of *Juneau* (CL-52). Named for the capital of Alaska, *Juneau* was laid down 27 May 1940 at the same New Jersey yard where *Atlanta* was constructed. Sponsored at her launch on 25 October 1941 by Mrs. Harry I. Lucas, wife of the mayor of Juneau, the cruiser was commissioned 14 February 1942 with Capt. Lyman K. Swenson commanding. Like *Atlanta*'s Captain Jenkins, Captain Swenson was *Juneau*'s only commanding officer, but unlike Captain Jenkins, Captain Swenson went down with his ship.

The first assignment for *Juneau* was blockade duty of Vichy French ships at Martinique and Guadaloupe in May 1942. Following patrol and escort duties in the Caribbean and North Atlantic for most of the summer, the cruiser steamed to the South Pacific. The crew of the ill-fated cruiser saw the loss of carrier *Wasp* (CV-7) on 15 September and had an opportunity to strike back in the 26 October 1942 Battle of Santa Cruz. Despite some good shooting, bad luck again attended the cruiser as her charge, carrier *Hornet* (CV-8), was sunk in this action.

Juneau's next-to-last mission was the successful escort of reinforcements to Guadalcanal between 8-12 November. On the afternoon of the 12th, *Juneau* and other American ships fought off an air attack against the newly arrived convoy and in this action *Juneau*'s gunners helped down six enemy aircraft. After dark *Juneau*, *Atlanta* and *Helena* joined heavy cruisers *San Francisco* and *Portland* and eight destroyers to challenge Japanese battleships, cruisers and destroyers heading into the area to bombard American positions on Guadalcanal. Just after midnight (13 November 1942) the first of the three great encounters of the three-day Naval Battle of Guadalcanal began (see *Portland* and *Atlanta* for other details of this battle). Soon into the confused, close-quarter fighting, *Juneau* took a torpedo on the port side and withdrew. Of necessity, attention was directed to saving the ship for another fight on another day. But it was not to be. The *Juneau* was down 12 feet by the bow and steaming on one screw at 13 knots as she moved toward safety and repair along with damaged *San Francisco* and others. Submarine-fired torpedoes headed for the two wounded American cruisers. All missed *San Francisco*, but one hit *Juneau* on the port side under the bridge at nearly the same location as the hit 10 hours earlier. Detonation of the torpedo apparently set off the forward magazines and the cruiser disintegrated in a terrific explosion. So catastrophic was the blast that other American ships in the formation continued on without stopping to search for survivors.

It is believed that nearly 100 men of the cruiser's crew somehow survived the blast, but poor communication delayed a rescue mission. Only 10 men subsequently lived to tell the story of *Juneau*'s last moments. Lost among the 700-member crew were the five Sullivan brothers. Their fate led to a change in naval policy regarding assignment of brothers to the same ship. This policy was the ship's legacy as was the naming of another cruiser of the same type in her memory, (*Juneau* [CL-119]) which won five battle stars for Korean War service. Another ship was named *The Sullivans* (DD-537) in honor of the five brothers lost with the first *Juneau*.

Juneau **photographed just after her 14 February 1942 commissioning. A censor has heavily retouched the photograph.**
USN

All five of the Sullivan brothers were lost when *Juneau* went down 13 November 1942. Their fate led to a policy change in assigning brothers to the same ship, and *The Sullivans* (DD-537) was named to honor their memory.   USN

SAN DIEGO CL-53

San Diego is seen here in her primary role as an escort for carriers such as the *Essex*-class carrier in the background. Early problems of insufficient directors for anti-aircraft defense by her 5-inch guns had been overcome by the date of this picture in late 1944.   USN

(15 Battle Stars) Named for the city in southern California, *San Diego* (CL-53) was laid down 27 March 1940 by Bethlehem Steel Co. of Quincy, Mass. Sponsored at her launch on 26 July 1941 by Mrs. Percy J. Benbough, the cruiser was commissioned 10 January 1942 with Capt. Benjamin F. Perry in command.

San Diego was one of the very few fortunate ships to fight through most of the Pacific war without receiving any major damage. She never fought in a major surface battle, but was at the side of carriers in the October 1942 Battle of Santa Cruz and the June 1944 Battle of the Philippine Sea. She spent so much time at sea after she was ready for combat in May 1942 that she did not receive 40mm guns in place of her original 1.1-inch anti-aircraft guns until December 1943.

On only a few occasions did *San Diego* close on enemy-held territory for shore bombardment. The vast majority of her time was spent protecting carriers as they moved relentlessly across the Pacific. After serving in most of the major campaigns of late 1942 through the end of the war and having steamed over a quarter-million miles, *San Diego* was decommissioned in November 1946, stricken on 1 March 1959 and sold for scrap.

It is somewhat sad that this ship, a ship that was "almost always there," is historically overlooked because of her good fortune. It is often stated that people remember the best and the worst, the victors and vanquished, but seldom remember those in the middle or the plodders. *San Diego* was a "plodder," a successful ship, but she was also a ship without wounds, and without a dramatic record. Therefore she is largely forgotten when the history of World War II is written.

SAN JUAN CL-54

(13 Battle Stars) Named for the city in Puerto Rico, *San Juan* (CL-54) was laid down 15 May 1940 in the same yard that built sister ship *San Diego*. Sponsored at her launch on 6 September 1941 by Mrs. Margarita Coll de Santori, the cruiser was commissioned 28 February 1942 with Capt. James E. Maher commanding.

First action for *San Juan* occurred during the initial landings in the Solomons. On 7 August 1942 the new cruiser provided gunfire support for the invading Marines and then devoted her energies to carrier protection. Having missed the Battle of the Eastern Solomons, *San Juan* steamed with *Portland* and battleship *South Dakota* to defend *Enterprise* in the crucial 26 October 1942 Battle of Santa Cruz. Although the carrier was the main attraction to enemy pilots, the last wave from the enemy flat-top *Junyo* fell upon *South Dakota* and *San Juan* as well as on the *Enterprise*. *San Juan* took one armor-piercing bomb which passed through the bottom of the cruiser before exploding and damaging the steering gear.

San Juan continued operations in the Solomons for most of 1943 before moving on to protect the new *Essex* (CV-9) during a raid on the Marshalls in December 1943. In 1944 the cruiser steamed alongside several of the newer carriers as the pace of invasion and occupation quickened across the Central Pacific. Success in the Carolines, Marianas and Philippines led to the final attacks in 1945 on Iwo Jima and Okinawa. Present at all these major battle sites, *San Juan* ended the war off the Japanese home islands. After "Magic Carpet" duty the veteran warship was decommissioned 9 November 1946. She was stricken from the Navy list 1 March 1959 and sold for scrap 31 October 1961.

With her crew at general quarters, *San Juan* awaits enemy planes during the October 1942 Battle of Santa Cruz. Note flash gear on the men and 5-inch and 1.1-inch guns ready for action. USN

OAKLAND CL-95

(9 Battle Stars) Named for the city in California, *Oakland* (CL-95) was laid down by Bethlehem Steel of San Francisco on 15 July 1941. Sponsored by Dr. Aurelia H. Reinhardt at the launch on 23 October 1942, the cruiser was commissioned 17 July 1943 with Capt. William K. Phillips commanding.

The first unit of the "late" *Atlanta* class, *Oakland* first entered combat in November 1943 by screening carriers in the Marshalls-Gilberts operation. Throughout 1944 and 1945 *Oakland* kept the barrels hot of her twelve 5-inch guns and her twenty-four 40mm and sixteen 20mm guns while fighting enemy air attacks against the carriers she was assigned to defend. After the Marshalls-Gilberts campaign the cruiser fought in the Marianas,

Carolines, Philippines, Bonins and Ryukyus before arriving off the coasts of the enemy home islands. Heavily engaged in the Okinawa Campaign, the cruiser was fortunate not to be a target for kamikazes, but she was only a short distance from *Bunker Hill* and *Enterprise* when they were hit.

At the end of the war *Oakland* made a "Magic Carpet" run to San Francisco, participated in the Navy Day ceremonies in her namesake city and then went into drydock for overhaul. After operating in the postwar Navy as a fleet gunnery training ship, the cruiser was decommissioned 1 July 1949 and was sold for scrap 1 December 1959.

Oakland at Mare Island Navy Yard 27 October 1943. Note locations of intermediate anti-aircraft guns.   USN

RENO CL-96

(3 Battle Stars) Named for the city in Nevada, *Reno* (CL-96) was laid down 1 August 1941 by Bethlehem Steel of San Francisco. Sponsored by Mrs. August C. Frohlich at the launch 23 December 1942, the cruiser was commissioned 28 December 1943. First commanding officer was Capt. Ralph C. Alexander who would be with *Reno* throughout her combat career.

Joining the Fifth Fleet in the spring of 1944, *Reno*'s first action was in the defense of carriers during the late-May raids against Marcus Island and Wake Island. A participant in the Battle of the Philippine Sea, *Reno* helped cover the taking of Saipan and Guam before moving in the fall to support operations in the Philippines. As part of the Philippine operation *Reno* moved with a force of carriers and screening ships to raid enemy airfields on Formosa 12-14 October 1944. In this strike *Reno*'s guns shot down six planes, but the ship had one bad moment when one of her victims crashed onto her near the stern. Damage was relatively light and the ship did not require the help of a major repair facility.

On 24 October *Reno* was with light carrier *Princeton* when the carrier was badly damaged by an enemy bomb. The cruiser helped rescue personnel from the burning carrier and helped fight fires. However, the explosion of the carrier's torpedo warheads sealed her fate and a destroyer—also with *Princeton* survivors on board—was ordered to sink the hulk with torpedoes. Of the six torpedoes fired by the destroyer only one hit and it was well forward. Two other torpedoes curved back toward the destroyer. With men aboard the destroyer in a frame of mind to mutiny, *Reno* was ordered to sink *Princeton*. The little-used torpedo tubes of the cruiser were equal to the task and the carrier disappeared after a tremendous blast tore her apart.

Violence similar to that suffered by *Princeton* came to *Reno* shortly thereafter. On 3 November *Reno* was struck by a submarine torpedo off San Bernardino Strait. Only two men were killed and only four were injured, but the cruiser was very seriously damaged. With power gone and high seas splashing across the aft portion of the ship, *Reno* had to be towed 700 miles to Ulithi. The war had ended by the time the cruiser was repaired in the United States, but the ship was needed for "Magic Carpet" duties. These completed, the cruiser was decommissioned 4 November 1946 and was sold for scrap 22 March 1962.

Leaking fuel oil and taking water after being hit by an enemy submarine torpedo 3 November 1944, *Reno* fights to survive.

USN

FLINT CL-97

(**4 Battle Stars**) Named for a city in Michigan, *Flint* (CL-97) was laid down 23 October 1942 by Bethlehem Steel of San Francisco. The cruiser was sponsored at her launch on 25 January 1944 by Mrs. R.A. Pitcher and was commissioned 31 August 1944 with Capt. C.R. Will in command.

Arriving for duty at Ulithi 27 December 1944, the cruiser first steamed into a combat area only days later when she was assigned to cover the invasion of Luzon in the Philippines. In the last eight months of the war *Flint*

added her protective anti-aircraft fire to carrier screens off Iwo Jima, Okinawa and the Japanese home islands. Joining in the final bombardment of the enemy home islands, *Flint* served as a rescue ship and homing station for transport planes bringing occupation troops to Japan. After "Magic Carpet" duty the cruiser was deactivated in January 1946, placed out of commission 6 May 1947 and held in reserve until stricken 1 September 1965 and scrapped.

Flint at San Francisco 18 September 1944 showing radar installations.   USN

TUCSON CL-98

(**1 Battle Star**) Named for the city in Arizona, *Tucson* (CL-98) was laid down 23 December 1942 at the same yard in San Francisco that built the earlier three *Oaklands*. Sponsored at her launch on 3 September 1944 by Mrs. Emmett S. Claunch Sr., the cruiser was commissioned 3 February 1945 with Capt. Arthur D. Ayrault commanding.

Tucson won only one battle star and that was for helping defend carriers during the final air attacks on the Japanese home islands. The new cruiser remained in the

Far East for occupation duty after the fall of Japan, but she was back at San Pedro, Calif. in time to take part in the late-October 1945 Navy Day celebrations. Being a latecomer, *Tucson* was not immediately deactivated. She served as an anti-aircraft gunnery training ship until August 1946, and then was overhauled and served as a command ship for destroyers. After an extensive cruise to the Far East, the ship was decommissioned 11 June 1949. Stricken 1 June 1966 she served as a test hulk and was then sold for scrap 24 February 1971.

THE CLEVELAND CLASS

INITIALLY AUTHORIZED BY THE BILL IN 1934 THAT provided for the replacement of overage warships, the first units of the *Cleveland* class were not funded until 1939. The naval expansion legislation approved in 1940 added additional units and this class became the largest single cruiser class in the history of the United States Navy. Twenty-two members of this class won battle stars (see table) and their collective total was 132, far more than any other cruiser class. This, of course, would be expected in view of the disparity of units. An additional seven members of the class were completed in late 1944 and 1945 but did not win any battle stars. Nine other hulls intended to be cruisers were converted into fast, light aircraft carriers (CVLs) and eight further hulls were authorized but were cancelled in November 1945.

Cleveland-class Cruisers Awarded Battle Stars in World War II

CL-55	Cleveland	13	Navy Unit Commendation
CL-56	Columbia	10	Navy Unit Commendation
CL-57	Montpelier	13	Navy Unit Commendation
CL-58	Denver	11	Navy Unit Commendation
CL-60	Santa Fe	13	Navy Unit Commendation
CL-62	Birmingham	9	Navy Unit Commendation
CL-63	Mobile	11	
CL-64	Vincennes	6	
CL-65	Pasadena	5	
CL-66	Springfield	2	
CL-67	Topeka	2	3 Battle Stars, Vietnam
CL-80	Biloxi	9	
CL-81	Houston	3	
CL-86	Vicksburg	2	
CL-87	Duluth	2	
CL-89	Miami	6	
CL-90	Astoria	5	
CL-91	Oklahoma City	2	13 Battle Stars, Vietnam
CL-101	Amsterdam	1	
CL-103	Wilkes-Barre	4	
CL-104	Atlanta	2	
CL-105	Dayton	1	

Cleveland-class Cruisers Completed, No Battle Stars in World War II

CL-82	Providence	CL-102	Portsmouth
CL-83	Manchester	CL-106	Fargo*
CL-92	Little Rock	CL-107	Huntington*
CL-93	Galveston		

Fargo and *Huntington* were officially grouped with the Cleveland class but differed slightly by having only one stack. Unofficially, these two ships are often referred to as the "Fargo class."

Cleveland-class Cruisers Authorized but Cancelled 11 August 1945

CL-94	Youngstown	CL-111	Wilmington
CL-108	Newark	CL-116	Tallahassee
CL-109	New Haven	CL-117	Cheyenne

CL-110	Buffalo	CL-118	Chattanooga

The *Clevelands* essentially were modernized *Brooklyns* and similarities were found in dimensions, armament, propulsion and overall appearance. The more notable differences were in the number and arrangement of 6-inch turrets and cruising range. Too, the *Clevelands* were in many ways similar to the heavy cruiser *Baltimore* class.

One considerable difference between the new *Clevelands* and the *Brooklyn-Helena* classes was cost. Whereas the *Brooklyns* and *Helenas* cost approximately $19 million, the *Clevelands* price tags ranged from approximately $31 million for the 1939 units to over $42 million for late-war members. Complement was similar, however, as both classes carried 1,200 officers and men during the war. Overall length of the *Clevelands* was 610 feet, beam was 63 feet and draft was 20 feet average and 24 feet maximum. Displacement was 10,000 tons standard and 13,100 tons when ready for combat. Designed to achieve 33 knots, most of these ships registered 32 knots on trial and closer to 30 knots during combat operations. A continuing need for new equipment, especially anti-aircraft guns, gun directors and newer radar, added weight to ships of all types as the war progressed. This factor adversely affected speed. Horsepower for this class was 100,000, while each cruiser had four screws and carried 2,498 tons of fuel which provided a cruising radius of 5,600 miles at 25 knots or 9,900 miles at 15 knots.

Protection for the *Clevelands* was only slightly better than the *Brooklyns* and nearly the same as the *Helenas*. Side armor, which covered over 400 feet, ranged from 1.5 inches to 5 inches, deck armor was 3 inches plus 2 inches and turret armor ranged from 3 to 5 inches. Aircraft provisions were the same as the *Brooklyns* and *Helenas* with two catapults aft served by one crane and the two to four scout planes maintained in the built-in fantail hangar.

The single significant distinguishing characteristic between the *Clevelands* and the preceding *Brooklyn-Helena* classes was the arrangement of the *Clevelands'* 6-inch guns in four triple turrets, two forward and two aft. This weight-saving arrangement allowed the *Clevelands* to carry more 5-inch dual-purpose rifles (12 instead of 8). As none of the *Clevelands* arrived in combat before the summer of 1942, when they did arrive they came with 40mm and 20mm guns as original intermediate and close-in weapons. The *Clevelands'* 40mm barrels ranged from 16 to 28, and 20mm placements ranged from 10 to 23.

Most of the combat-active *Clevelands* were decommissioned soon after the war, but some were converted to missile cruisers and served as part of the U.S. Navy's first generation of electronic-warfare ships. None of the 22 combat-active *Clevelands* of World War II saw any service in Korea although two, *Oklahoma City* and *Topeka*, saw service off Vietnam.

(13 Battle Stars, Navy Unit Commendation) Like many of the other leaders of the respective cruiser classes, *Cleveland* (CL-55) compiled a particularly distinguished war record. Laid down 1 July 1940 at the New York Shipbuilding Corp. yard in Camden, N.J., the cruiser was launched 1 November 1941 with Mrs. H. Burton rendering christening honors. *Cleveland* was commissioned 15 June 1942 with Capt. E.W. Burrough commanding and the ship quickly departed on her shakedown cruise.

In November 1942 *Cleveland* began her combat service off North Africa in support of the Allied invasion. Two months later the cruiser was in the Pacific to help replace the void left by the loss of seven cruisers in the first three months of the fight for Guadalcanal. Ironically, in her first Pacific action *Cleveland* was part of the American force off the Rennell Islands when *Chicago* (CA-29) became the eighth cruiser to be lost.

As the Allied thrust began in the central Solomons, *Cleveland* became very active with two actions being particularly noteworthy. On 6 March 1943 *Cleveland* bombarded enemy airfields at Vila and afterward the cruiser along with *Denver* (CL-58), *Montpelier* (CL-57) and three destroyers caught Japanese destroyers *Minegumo* and *Murasame* and sank them. On 1-2 November *Cleveland*, *Montpelier*, *Columbia* (CL-56), *Denver* and eight destroyers carried out two bombardments in support of the invasion of Bougainville and then fought off a Japanese force of four cruisers and six destroyers in the Battle of Empress Augusta Bay. This battle was reminiscent of the August 1942 Savo Island action in that the Japanese plan was to attack American transports during the night as they were still unloading at Cape Torokina. The outcome of this battle was much happier for the U.S. Navy than was the Savo Island fray as no American ship was lost while the Japanese lost light cruiser *Sendai* and destroyer *Hatsukaze*. American tactics had come a long way since August 1942. In this battle, destroyers were not tied to the cruisers; instead they made an independent torpedo attack before the cruisers opened fire. For her role in this battle *Cleveland* was awarded the Navy Unit Commendation.

Cleveland remained in the Solomons and southwest Pacific while many of her sister ships fought in the central Pacific (Marshalls-Gilberts) but she was with them for the Marianas operations in the summer of 1944, and she fought in the Battle of the Philippine Sea. Missing the early stages of the Philippine campaign due to overhaul, the cruiser was on hand in February 1945 to aid in the consolidation of American gains in those islands; except for brief assignments at Borneo in June and Okinawa in late July and early August 1945, she spent the last six months of the war in the Philippines. After brief occupation duty in the fall, the cruiser was overhauled and used as a training ship until deactivated in the summer of 1946. Decommissioned in February 1947, the ship was in reserve until sold for scrap 18 February 1960.

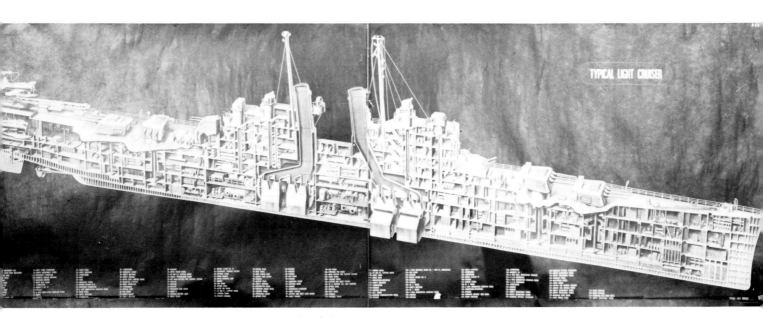

This drawing shows the design of the *Cleveland*-class cruisers. USN

Construction goes forward on class leader *Cleveland* at the Camden, N.J., New York Ship-building Corp. on New Year's Day 1942.   USN

The new *Cleveland* in late 1942 just before entering combat service. *Cleveland* was the first of 22 class members to fight in World War II. Seven other units were completed after the war, eight planned units were cancelled and nine other hulls were converted into light carriers (CVLs).   USN

COLUMBIA CL-56

(10 Battle Stars, Navy Unit Commendation) Named for the capital city of South Carolina, *Columbia* (CL-56) was laid down 19 August 1940 by the New York Shipbuilding Corp. Sponsored at her launch on 17 December 1941 by Miss J.A. Paschal, the cruiser was commissioned 29 July 1942 with Capt. W.A. Heard commanding.

After a hurried shakedown cruise *Columbia* sailed for the South Pacific and was initiated into combat along with sister ships *Cleveland* and *Montpelier* in the Battle of Rennell Island. In the spring and summer of 1943 the cruiser patrolled and carried out bombardment missions in the central Solomons before steaming to Australia for overhaul. On 2 November 1943 *Columbia* was with the other three first units of her class (*Cleveland, Montpelier*

and *Denver*) in the Battle of Empress Augusta Bay (see *Cleveland* for details) in which the Japanese lost a light cruiser and destroyer. In early 1944 *Columbia* remained in the southwest Pacific to provide relief for forces in that region while the major push across the central Pacific was beginning in the Marshalls and Gilberts. In September 1944 the cruiser supported landings in the Palaus, particularly the taking of Peleliu, and steamed the following month for raids in the Philippines in preparation for the main assault. With the old battleships during the Surigao Strait action in the Battle of Leyte Gulf, *Columbia* had the satisfaction of fighting in the last major battleship engagement of the war, and probably the last ever.

On 6 January 1945 *Columbia* was in Lingayen Gulf for

A Japanese kamikaze dives on *Columbia* at 1729 hours, 6 January 1945, off the Philippines.
USN

Explosion from kamikaze hit on *Columbia*. Thirteen were killed in this attack on 6 January 1945 and three days later the cruiser was hit by another kamikaze with 24 killed.   USN

pre-invasion bombardment duty when she was struck by a Japanese suicide plane in one of the first kamikaze attacks. Hit on the port quarter, the ship caught on fire, lost the use of her two aft 6-inch turrets and suffered casualties of 13 killed and 44 wounded. Remaining on station, the cruiser continued her bombardment mission with available guns while damage control parties worked to repair her wounds. Only three days later, *Columbia* still on station, was hit by another kamikaze and suffered another 24 killed and 97 wounded. Again, the ship's crew patched holes, checked flooding, extinguished fires and continued to provide bombardment and fire support. For completing her assigned mission in Lingayen Gulf despite

damage and casualties, *Columbia* received the Navy Unit Commendation.

Departing the Philippines for repairs, overhaul and replacement of personnel, the cruiser was away from the war until June 1945 when she reported again to the Philippines. The cruiser finished her war service by supporting operations on Borneo and searching for enemy shipping in the East China Sea. After a brief period of transporting troops, the ship steamed to Philadelphia in December 1945, was overhauled and served as a training ship for the Naval Reserve until 1 July 1946. Decommissioned 30 November 1946, *Columbia* was sold for scrap 18 February 1959.

MONTPELIER CL-57

Montpelier at Mare Island 21 October 1944. Although the war in the Pacific would last nearly one more year, *Montpelier* had already been awarded the Navy Unit Commendation by the date of this photo.   USN

(13 Battle Stars, Navy Unit Commendation) - Named for the capital city of Vermont, *Montpelier* (CL-57) was laid down 2 December 1940 by the New York Shipbuilding Corp. Sponsored at her launch on 12 February 1942 by Mrs. William F. Corry, the cruiser was commissioned 9 September 1942 with Capt. Leighton Wood in command.

Montpelier was a lucky ship as she gave the enemy many opportunities to hurt her but was never severely damaged. In addition to good fortune, *Montpelier* also enjoyed success thanks to good leadership and an effective crew. She was often the flagship for the cruiser divisions in which she served and was the flagship for the American victory in the 2 November 1943 Battle of Em-

press Augusta Bay. *Montpelier* also fought in the Battle of Rennell Island 29 January 1943 and the Battle of the Philippine Sea 19-20 June 1944. Often in company with the other three early units of the *Cleveland* class, *Montpelier* fought numerous actions in the central Solomons and Bismarcks before moving on to the campaigns in the Marianas and Philippines. The cruiser concluded her service with the invasion of Borneo in the summer of 1945 and three anti-shipping sweeps in the East China Sea. After brief occupation duty *Montpelier* transferred to the Atlantic Fleet and served until decommissioned 24 January 1947. Struck from the Naval Register 1 March 1959, the ship was sold for scrap 22 January 1960.

DENVER CL-58

(11 Battle Stars, Navy Unit Commendation) Named for the capital city of Colorado, *Denver* (CL-58) was laid down 26 December 1940 by the New York Shipbuilding Corp. Sponsored at her launch on 4 April 1942 by Miss L.J. Stapleton, the cruiser was commissioned 15 October 1942 with Capt. R.B. Carney comman-

ding.

First combat for *Denver* was the 6 March 1943 bombardment of Vila on the island of Kolombangara and the night surface action which cost the enemy two destroyers. On 2 November 1943 *Denver* joined *Cleveland, Montpelier* and *Columbia* and eight destroyers to sink a light

This May 1944 photograph of the aft section of *Denver* provides considerable detail. Note the aircraft hangar and catapults.   USN

cruiser and destroyer in the Battle of Empress Augusta Bay (see *Cleveland* for details of both actions). *Denver* was the only American cruiser to incur damage in the Empress Augusta Bay fight as she took three 8-inch shells. Fortunately, all three shells failed to explode, but they did cause some flooding. Less than two weeks later, however, *Denver* was hit by an aerial torpedo in her aft engine room and suffered casualties of 20 killed and 11 wounded. For her conduct in these actions *Denver* received the Navy Unit Commendation.

Denver was away from the war for repairs until June 1944 after her wounding on 13 November. First duty upon return was to steam with a force to raid and neutralize enemy bases in the Bonins and Marianas in preparation for the invasion of the latter. In September *Denver* supported the invasion of the Palaus, moving close to enemy-held positions to cover minesweeping and under-

water demolition operations. In October she provided these same functions as American forces moved into the Philippines. The cruiser interrupted her bombardment duties to join other units in the celebrated "big gun" action in Surigao Strait on 24 October. After the Battle of Leyte Gulf the cruiser remained in the gulf to defend American ships, and more than once she took light casualties as enemy planes crashed close aboard. Remaining in the Philippines for most of the rest of the war, *Denver* did leave long enough to support the invasion of Borneo in June 1945 and to make an anti-shipping sweep off Okinawa in July and early August. After covering the landing of occupation forces, *Denver* sailed to Norfolk, Va. for overhaul and then made several short cruises before being decommissioned 7 February 1947. Thirteen years later, on 29 February 1960, *Denver* was sold and scrapped.

SANTA FE CL-60

(13 Battle Stars, Navy Unit Commendation) Named for the capital city of New Mexico, *Santa Fe* (CL-60) was laid down 7 June 1941 at New York Shipbuilding's Camden, N.J., yard. Sponsored at the launch on 19 June 1942 by Miss Caroline T. Chavez, the cruiser was commissioned 24 November 1942 with Capt. Russell Berkey in command.

Santa Fe was a very successful and active ship in her 28 months of war service. The cruiser's first assignment was in the Aleutians. During her five months there she bombarded Attu, patrolled, bombarded Kiska on raids and then supported the August 1943 landings. In the fall of 1943 *Santa Fe* screened carriers as the big thrust toward Japan began. In the months that followed the cruiser de-

fended carriers and/or bombarded enemy positions at Tarawa, Wake, Bougainville, Kwjalein, Wotje, Truk, Emirau, Palau, Yap, Woleai, Hollandia, Ponape, Saipan, Tinian, Guam, Peleliu, the Philippines, Iwo Jima and Okinawa.

Several actions highlighted the combat career of *Santa Fe*. On the night of 20 June 1944 she was part of the force that experienced the exhilaration of lighting the night for returning carrier planes after the Marianas "Turkey Shoot" and chase. She was with *Mobile* (see for details), *Biloxi* and *Oakland* on 4 August 1944 when they and several destroyers caught a small enemy convoy and sank three ships. For four days in October 1944 (13-17) she helped defend damaged *Canberra* and *Houston* as they

With 13 battle stars, *Santa Fe*, shown here near the end of the war, tied *Cleveland* and *Montpelier* for most battle stars within their class.

USN

were towed to safety, and off Cape Engano on 25 October 1944 *Santa Fe* had the pleasure of finishing off enemy carrier *Chiyoda* and destroyer *Hatsuzuki* which had been disabled by American carrier planes. However, like the experiences of *Birmingham* and *Wilkes-Barre*, *Santa Fe* might be best remembered for the three hours she bumped alongside the fire-consumed carrier *Franklin* (CV-13) on 19 March 1945. For her firefighting and rescue efforts on behalf of *Franklin*, *Santa Fe* was awarded the Navy Unit Commendation.

Overdue for a trip to a Navy Yard and in need of repairs after her experience with *Franklin*, *Santa Fe* steamed to San Pedro, Calif. She was ready for duty again in August 1945 and was en route to Wake Island for a raid when the war ended. Occupation duty was followed by "Magic Carpet" runs and on 19 October 1946 the war-worn cruiser was decommissioned. After 13 years in mothballs the cruiser was sold for scrap 9 November 1959.

BIRMINGHAM CL-62

(9 Battle Stars, Navy Unit Commendation) Most of the *Cleveland*-class cruisers that were active in combat zones finished the war with little damage and few casualties, and none were lost. However, not all the *Clevelands* were lucky; perhaps the most unlucky member of the class was *Birmingham* (CL-62). It seemed that she was a magnet in drawing steel to her.

Named for the old steel city in central Alabama, *Birmingham* was laid down 17 February 1941 by the Newport News Shipbuilding and Dry Dock Co. Sponsored at her launch on 20 March 1942 by Mrs. W. Cooper Green, the cruiser was commissioned 29 January 1943 with Capt. J. Wilkes in command.

Birmingham began her wartime experience in the Mediterranean by providing gunfire support during the 10-26 July 1943 invasion of Sicily. Reassigned to the Pacific, the cruiser screened carriers as their planes raided Tarawa (18 September 1943) and Wake Island (5-6 October 1943). In the action off Empress Augusta Bay 8-9 November 1943 *Birmingham* absorbed the first of her numerous wounds when she was hit by one torpedo and two bombs. She was out of the war for repairs until late February 1944. The cruiser returned to action in the Pacific where she supported the invasion of Saipan, Tinian and Guam; took part in the 19-20 June Battle of the Philippine Sea; steamed to raid the Philippines, Okinawa and Formosa; and then fought in the Battle of Leyte Gulf. During the Battle of Leyte Gulf on 24 October

Birmingham at sea 20 February 1943 soon after commissioning.   USN

1944 *Birmingham* spent several hours fighting fires alongside *Princeton* in an attempt to save the burning carrier. However, a tremendous explosion shattered the carrier and ripped the superstructure of the cruiser. Two hundred thirty-seven of *Birmingham*'s crew died and 426 were injured.

Again the crew returned to San Francisco for repairs and new personnel. Back into combat five months later, *Birmingham* supported the invasion of Iwo Jima and Okinawa. While off Okinawa on 4 May 1945 the cruiser was hit for the third and last time when a kamikaze struck the ship near turret number two. Fifty-one were killed and 81 wounded.

Repaired only days before the war's end, *Birmingham* returned to a peaceful Pacific for occupation duty before being placed out of commission 2 January 1947. The cruiser remained in reserve until stricken from the Navy list 1 March 1959 and scrapped.

Birmingham alongside the burning *Princeton* during the 24 October 1944 Battle of Leyte Gulf. Before the sun set on this day the carrier went down, but not before an explosion aboard her killed 237 men on *Birmingham* as the cruiser was fighting *Princeton's* fires.　　　USN

Burned and battered after her experience with *Princeton*, *Birmingham* returns to San Francisco for repairs and personnel replacements.　　　USN

MOBILE CL-63

(11 Battle Stars) Named for the coastal city in southern Alabama, *Mobile* (CL-63) was laid down 14 April 1941 by Newport News Shipbuilding and Dry Dock Co. Sponsored at the launch on 15 May 1942 by Mrs. Harry T. Hartwell, the cruiser was commissioned 24 March 1943 with Capt. Charles J. Wheeler commanding.

She began her wartime service as part of the 22 August 1943 raid on Marcus Island, and *Mobile* participated in all the major operations of the last two years of the war except the invasion of Iwo Jima. Iwo was missed because of overhaul, but between August 1943 and August 1945 *Mobile* fought through the Gilberts, Marshalls, Carolines, Marianas, Palaus, Bonins, Philippines and Ryukyus.

Highlights of *Mobile*'s career were her participation in the Battle of the Philippine Sea 19-20 June 1944; the 13-16 October 1944 battle off Formosa when *Mobile* helped screen "CripDiv 1" (*Canberra* and *Houston*) as TF 38 tried to lure Japanese surface units into battle; and the 25 October action off Cape Engano—one of the four actions comprising the Battle of Leyte Gulf—when *Mobile* took part in the sinking of enemy units previously damaged by carrier planes.

The brief surface action off Cape Engano was not *Mobile*'s only opportunity to use her 6-inch guns against enemy ships. On 6 October 1944 she and two destroyers sank a large cargo ship off the Philippines. Before that action, on 4 August 1944 *Mobile* teamed with *Santa Fe*, *Biloxi*, *Oakland* and several destroyers to attack an enemy convoy in the Bonin Islands. The quickly assembled assault team was detached and sent forward to catch the enemy ships that had been spotted by carrier planes. At the end of the day the American cruiser-destroyer group sank a destroyer, oiler and cargo ship. Before leaving the area after midnight, the American ships shelled Chichi Jima harbor with excellent results.

Mobile was off Okinawa for two months providing gunfire support, screening carriers against the heaviest concentration of kamikaze attacks in the war, and searching for enemy submarines and suicide boats. Occupation duty and "Magic Carpet" runs completed the service career of the cruiser. Decommissioned 9 May 1947, *Mobile* was sold for scrap 16 December 1959.

Mobile at Norfolk, Va., 14 April 1943.   USN

VINCENNES CL-64

(6 Battle Stars) Originally named *Flint*, CL-64 was renamed *Vincennes* on 16 October 1942 to perpetuate the name of the heavy cruiser lost in the August Battle of Savo Island. Laid down 7 March 1942 at Bethlehem Shipbuilding's plant at Quincy, Mass., the cruiser was launched 17 July 1943. On hand to christen the ship was Mrs. Arthur A. Osborn, the former Miss Harriet V. Kimmell, who had also sponsored the lost *Vincennes* (CA-44). On 21 January 1944 the new cruiser was commissioned with Capt. Arthur D. Brown in command.

The second cruiser to carry the name of the city in Indiana was a much luckier ship than the first. Although constantly in combat from June 1944 until mid-June 1945, the new *Vincennes* was never seriously damaged. Screening duties and shore bombardment were the major contributions of the cruiser through the Marianas, Bonins, Ryukyus and Philippines. Heavily involved in gunfire support off Okinawa for a month, *Vincennes* was ordered back to the United States for a much-needed overhaul in late-June 1945. When the war ended the cruiser was still at San Francisco, but she returned to the Pacific for "Magic Carpet" runs. Decommissioned 10 September 1946, the ship was struck from the Navy list on 1 April 1966 and was sunk as a target in missile experiments.

Port view in 1944 of the second *Vincennes* (CL-64), which inherited the name of the heavy cruiser lost at Savo Island in 1942.   USN

PASADENA CL-65

(5 Battle Stars) Named for the Rose Bowl city in California, *Pasadena* (CL-65) was laid down 6 February 1943 by Bethlehem Steel of Quincy, Mass. Sponsored at her launch on 28 December 1943 by Mrs. C.G. Wopschall, the cruiser was commissioned 8 June 1944 with Capt. Richard B. Tuggle commanding.

Pasadena arrived in the Philippines in November 1944 to begin her combat service. Primary responsibility for the new cruiser was defense against air attack, but her guns were added to the bombardment force off Iwo Jima in February 1945. In her 10 months of war, *Pasadena* steamed from the southeastern tip of Indochina to northern Japan with many stops in between. The cruiser was active in bombardments on the Ryukyus and screened carriers during the invasion of Okinawa and the July air raids against the enemy home islands.

On occupation duty until January 1946, *Pasadena* thereafter returned to San Pedro, Calif. for overhaul. Returning to the Pacific, the cruiser exercised with other units of the fleet until decommissioned 12 January 1950. In reserve at Bremerton for 20 years, the cruiser was finally broken up for scrap in 1971.

Bow view of *Pasadena* in 1944. Note effect of camouflage on turret tops and deck.   USN

SPRINGFIELD CL-66

(2 Battle Stars) One of only three ships of the *Cleveland* class to win battle stars in World War II and later be converted into a guided-missile cruiser, *Springfield* (CL-66) was laid down 13 February 1943 by Bethlehem Steel in Quincy, Mass. Named for a host of American cities that are named Springfield, the cruiser was co-sponsored by Mrs. Angelina Bertera and Miss Norma McCurley at the launch 9 March 1944. Commissioned 9 September 1944, the new cruiser began her maiden voyage two months later with Capt. Felix L. Johnson commanding.

She was part of an escort for President Roosevelt during his journey to the Yalta Conference in January 1945,

and *Springfield* soon after steamed through the Panama Canal on her way to Pearl Harbor. In the late spring and early summer *Springfield* helped screen carriers off Okinawa and Japan and also took part in shore bombardment. After the war the cruiser operated along the West Coast of the United States and in the Far East until decommissioned in January 1950.

After seven years in reserve *Springfield* was towed from San Francisco to Massachusetts for conversion into a guided-missile cruiser. Rebuilt, the cruiser was redesignated CLG-7 and was recommissioned 2 July 1960. Very little similarity existed between CLG-7 and her appearance as CL-66. An enlarged superstructure housed the electronics necessary for the launching of up to 120 Terrier missiles and also provided space necessary for her to serve as a flagship. All light anti-aircraft guns were removed, 5-inch guns were reduced from 12 barrels to two and only the forward-most 6-inch triple turret was retained.

After extensive service in the Atlantic and Mediterranean, *Springfield* was again decommissioned 15 May 1974 and was sold for scrap 31 July 1978.

TOPEKA CL-67

(2 Battle Stars in World War II, 3 Battle Stars for Vietnam Service) One of the only two *Cleveland*-class light cruisers to see action in both World War II and Vietnam, *Topeka* (CL-67), named for the city in Kansas, was laid down 21 April 1943 at the Bethlehem Steel Co. in Quincy, Mass. Sponsored at her launch on 19 August 1944 by Mrs. Frank J. Warren, the new cruiser was commissioned 23 December 1944 with Capt. Thomas Wattles commanding.

Topeka's World War II combat career was limited to the last strikes against the Ryukyus and the Japanese home islands in June-August 1945. During those three months the cruiser provided shore bombardment and anti-aircraft defense for carriers. After the war *Topeka* remained in the Pacific for occupation duty and local operations until decommissioned 18 June 1949.

In 1957 *Topeka*, like sister ship *Springfield*, was towed from San Francisco to the East Coast for conversion into a guided-missile cruiser. However, work on *Topeka* was done at the New York Navy Shipyard and there were differences in the two cruisers when completed. *Topeka* was similar to *Springfield* in most characteristics, but was not fitted as a flagship and therefore retained a greater portion of her original armament. *Topeka*, now CLG-8, emerged from conversion with her two forward 6-inch turrets and three forward 5-inch turrets still in place. Like *Springfield*, her Terrier missile launcher was aft.

Recommissioned 26 March 1960, *Topeka* was deployed to the Pacific where she completed three relatively quiet tours to the Far East. In late 1965, however, *Topeka*'s service life became quite eventful as she moved off the coast of Vietnam to add the weight of her 6-inch guns against communist positions and to defend carriers with her missiles. Too, the cruiser conducted search-and-rescue missions for downed air-crews. Overhauled in late 1966 and early 1967, the cruiser was assigned to the Mediterranean and completed most of her remaining active life there. Decommissioned 5 June 1969, *Topeka* was sold for scrap 20 March 1975.

BILOXI CL-80

Biloxi at Norfolk, Va., two weeks after her 31 August 1943 commissioning.

USN

(9 Battle Stars) Named for the coastal city in southern Mississippi, *Biloxi* (CL-80) was laid down 9 July 1941 at Newport News Shipbuilding and Dry Dock Co. The ship was sponsored at her launching by Mrs. Louis Braun and was commissioned 31 August 1943 with Capt. D.M. McCurl commanding.

Assigned to Cruiser Division 13 of the Pacific Fleet, *Biloxi*'s history is nearly the same as the other members of the famous division. In most of her operations *Biloxi* was in company with *Mobile, Santa Fe, Birmingham* and *Reno*. The cruiser was damaged off Okinawa 27 March 1945, but she was not hurt greatly enough to have to leave the area. From her first action in the Marshall Islands in

January 1944, *Biloxi* was continuously engaged until Japan's capitulation except for short periods when she was undergoing maintenance. In her 20 months of wartime service *Biloxi* fought through all the major island campaigns in the central and southwestern Pacific, and was involved in the last two major sea battles of the Pacific war—the battles of the Philippine Sea and Leyte Gulf. Like nearly all her sister ships that were heavily engaged in the last two years of the war, she was quickly deactivated at the end of hostilities. Decommissioned 18 May 1946, the ship remained in reserve until sold for scrap 1 September 1961.

HOUSTON CL-81

(3 Battle Stars) Hull CL-81 was originally named *Vicksburg* when laid down at Newport News 4 August 1941, but when the citizens of Houston, Texas, pledged subscriptions for war bonds to cover the cost of replacing the heavy cruiser (CA-30) lost in the Battle of the Java Sea, the name of CL-81 was changed to *Houston* on 12 October 1942. Sponsored at the launch on 19 June 1943 by Mrs. C.V. Hamill, the cruiser was commissioned 20 December 1943 with Capt. W.W. Behrens in command.

Houston screened carriers as their planes struck enemy positions near the Marianas in May and June 1944 in preparation for the invasion of Saipan, Guam and Tinian. The cruiser was present during the Battle of the Philippine Sea and before the end of June she was engaged in shore bombardment off Guam and Rota. In September the cruiser shelled Peleliu and in October she moved with a force to neutralize Formosa in preparation for the push into the Philippines. While engaged off Formosa

Battered by two aerial torpedoes in October 1944, *Houston* (CL-81) made a precarious voyage away from danger. Seen here in drydock, the cruiser did not complete repairs until after the war. NA

on 14 October, *Houston* was hit by an aerial torpedo and severely damaged. With power gone *Houston* was towed by *Boston* (CA-69), within sight of the similarly damaged *Canberra* (CA-70) which was also under tow. On the 16th, while still under tow (now by Navy tug *Pawnee*), the cruiser took another aerial torpedo on the starboard quarter. In danger of being lost after the first torpedo, the cruiser's condition was now critical. However, the damage control party still aboard refused to accept defeat and their heroic efforts and expertise kept the ship afloat until it arrived at Ulithi two weeks later. Casualties were relatively light for the amount of damage incurred: 55 were killed.

Stopping at several locations in the Pacific for temporary repairs and patching and strengthening, the cruiser finally ended her precarious voyage when she arrived at the New York Navy Yard 24 March 1945. Repaired after the end of the war, the ship returned to duty and took part in training exercises and goodwill cruises to Europe before being decommissioned 15 December 1947. On 1 March 1959 the cruiser that fought so hard to live was stricken and sold for scrap.

VICKSBURG CL-86

(**2 Battle Stars**) Originally named *Cheyenne* when laid down 26 October 1942 at the Newport News Shipbuilding and Dry Dock Co., the new cruiser had been renamed *Vicksburg* (CL-86) by the time she was launched on 14 December 1943. Christened by Miss Muriel Hamilton, the daughter of the mayor of Vicksburg, Miss., at the launch, the cruiser was completed 18 months later and was commissioned 12 June 1944. Capt. William C. Vose was the first commanding officer.

After serving as a pre-commissioning training vessel for newly formed crews, *Vicksburg* was assigned to the Pacific and first entered combat in February 1945 as she participated in the bombardment of Iwo Jima. Off Okinawa in the spring the cruiser's guns provided close support for advancing Army units. While many of her sister ships steamed off the coasts of the Japanese homeland in the summer of 1945, *Vicksburg* steamed off the coasts of the Philippines and China. At the close of hostilities *Vicksburg* became part of the "Magic Carpet" fleet. Decommissioned 30 June 1947 the ship was sold for scrap 25 August 1964.

DULUTH CL-87

(**2 Battle Stars**) Named for the city in Minnesota, *Duluth* (CL-87) was laid down 9 November 1942 at the Newport News Shipbuilding and Dry Dock Co. Sponsored at her launch on 13 January 1944 by Mrs. E. Hatch, wife of Duluth's mayor, the cruiser was commissioned 18 September 1944. First commanding officer was Capt. D.R. Osborn Jr.

Initial duty for *Duluth* was service as a training cruiser from December 1944 until 2 March 1945. Assigned to the Pacific, the cruiser joined the Fifth Fleet in May, but before encountering the enemy the ship's bow was severely damaged in a typhoon. After repairs *Duluth* helped screen carriers during the final strikes against the Japanese home islands. Brief occupation duty was followed by a happy journey to Seattle, Wash., for Navy Day celebrations before returning to assignments in the Pacific. Placed out of commission 25 July 1949, the cruiser was sold for scrap 14 November 1960.

MIAMI CL-89

(**6 Battle Stars**) Named for the city in southern Florida, *Miami* (CL-89) was laid down 2 August 1941 by Cramp of Philadelphia. Sponsored at her launch on 8 December 1942 by Mrs. C.H. Reeder, wife of Miami's mayor, the cruiser was commissioned 28 December 1943. First commanding officer was Capt. John G. Crawford.

Miami's combat career began in June 1944 as the U.S. Navy began the thrust into Japan's inner defenses. First was the Marianas campaign in June and July and then came the push into the Philippines in October 1944. In these operations *Miami* primarily screened carriers while her own spotter planes scouted and rescued downed American pilots. In one of the four major actions that comprised the Battle of Leyte Gulf, *Miami* sped north with Admiral Halsey to meet the enemy carriers off Cape Engano and returned with the force to catch and sink enemy destroyer *Nowaki* off San Bernadino Strait.

Unfortunately *Miami* was one of the ships caught in the infamous December 1944 typhoon in which three American destroyers were lost. Damaged herself by the storm, *Miami* nonetheless participated in the search for survivors. Continuing screening duties, the cruiser ranged up and down the Asian coast as her carriers raided enemy targets. After operating off Okinawa in the spring of 1945, the cruiser returned to San Francisco for overhaul in May and was still there when the war concluded. *Miami* returned to the Far East, accepted the surrender of several islands in the Ryukyus and inspected the damage at Truk, Japan's major naval base in the Carolines. Returning to the United States, the ship remained at sea until decommissioned 30 June 1947. She was sold for scrap 26 July 1962.

ASTORIA CL-90

(5 Battle Stars) Named for the heavy cruiser (CA-34) lost in the August 1942 Battle of Savo Island, *Astoria* (CL-90) was laid down 6 September 1941. Hull number CL-90 began life as *Wilkes-Barre* but was renamed *Astoria* 16 October 1942. The new cruiser was sponsored at her 6 March 1943 launch by Mrs. Robert Lucas and the ship was commissioned 17 May 1944 with Capt. G.C. Dyer in command.

Astoria screened carriers for the final nine months of the Pacific war and her anti-aircraft guns were active during the battles for Luzon, Iwo Jima, Okinawa and the summer raids against Japan. The cruiser's 6-inch and 5-inch guns assisted in the bombardments of the Bonins and Honshu. Remaining in the Pacific after the war until February 1949, the cruiser was decommissioned 1 July 1949 and rested in reserve until broken up for scrap in 1971.

OKLAHOMA CITY CL-91

(2 Battle Stars in World War II, 13 Battle Stars for Vietnam Service) One of two *Cleveland*-class light cruisers to see action in both World War II and Vietnam, *Oklahoma City* (CL-91) was laid down 8 December 1942 by the Cramp Shipbuilding Co. of Philadelphia. At her launch on 20 February 1944 the ship was sponsored by Mrs. Anton H. Classen. The cruiser was commissioned 22 December 1944 with Capt. C.B. Hunt commanding.

Oklahoma City operated in combat zones for the last three months of the war, and screened carriers and joined bombardment groups off the Ryukyus and Japanese home islands. After brief occupation duty, the cruiser returned to San Francisco where she was decommissioned 30 June 1947. Nearly 10 years later the cruiser was selected as one of six members of the *Cleveland* class to be converted to a guided-missile cruiser, and she joined former World War II steaming mates *Springfield* and *Topeka* in the new role. *Galveston* (CL-93), *Providence* (CL-82) and *Little Rock* (CL-92), all members of the *Cleveland* class, were also converted, but these three ships did not enter combat in World War II.

Oklahoma City's conversion was completed in August 1960 and she was recommissioned as CLG-5 on 7 September 1960. Fitted as a flagship, the cruiser retained only her forward-most 6-inch triple turret and one centerline 5-inch turret. Primary armament after conversion was the aft-mounted twin Talos surface-to-air launcher which could fire the 46 missiles carried by the ship. The first combat ship of the Pacific Fleet to successfully fire a Talos missile, *Oklahoma City* operated in the Far East from 1960 and was very active off Vietnam. During the Vietnam War *Oklahoma City* provided gunfire-support missions, screened carriers, sought for and rescued downed aircrews and served as Seventh Fleet flagship. Finally struck from the Navy list 15 December 1979, her eventual fate is pending.

AMSTERDAM CL-101

(1 Battle Star) Named for the city in New York, *Amsterdam* (CL-101) was laid down 3 March 1943 at Newport News Shipbuilding and Dry Dock Co. The original *Amsterdam* (CL-59) was converted to the light-carrier class-leader *Independence* (CVL-22). Sponsored at her launch on 25 April 1944 by Mrs. W.E. Hasenfuss, the cruiser was commissioned 8 January 1945 with Capt. A.P. Lawton in command.

Amsterdam's only battle action was with the Third Fleet in July and August 1945. As part of Cruiser Division 18 *Amsterdam* served in the screen for carriers as their planes flew the final strikes against Japan. Inactivated in January 1946, the ship was decommissioned 30 June 1947 and remained in reserve until broken up for scrap in 1971.

WILKES-BARRE CL-103

(4 Battle Stars) Named for the city in eastern Pennsylvania, *Wilkes-Barre* (CL-103) was laid down 14 December 1942 by the New York Shipbuilding Corp. Sponsored at her launch 24 December 1943 by Mrs. Grace S. Miner, the cruiser was commissioned 1 July 1944 with Capt. Robert L. Porter Jr. commanding.

Wilkes-Barre operated in combat zones for the final eight months of the war. The cruiser spent much of her time screening carriers during their neutralizing raids in support of the invasions of Iwo Jima and Okinawa, but she was also called upon for shore bombardment at Iwo and the southern coast of Honshu. A lucky ship, *Wilkes-Barre* did not suffer significant damage or casualties during her combat operations.

Wilkes-Barre will probably be better remembered than many of her sisters due to her firefighting role alongside *Bunker Hill* (CV-17) on 11 May 1945. Two kamikazes hit the big carrier and turned her aft flight deck and hangar deck into an inferno. For over four hours *Wilkes-Barre* stood by the burning carrier, fought fires and evacuated the wounded. The hazards of this type duty had been proven in the *Princeton-Birmingham* tragedy.

After occupation duty in the Far East and a short tour to Europe, *Wilkes-Barre* was decommissioned 9 October 1947 and struck from the Navy list 15 January 1971. Subjected to underwater explosive experiments off the Florida Keys, the cruiser broke apart with her after section sinking on 12 May 1972 and the forward section going under the following day.

Wilkes-Barre pulls alongside the burning carrier *Bunker Hill* on 11 May 1945. The hazards of this type of duty were well-known but disdained.   NA

ATLANTA CL-104

(2 Battle Stars) Named for the cruiser lost during the November 1942 Naval Battle of Guadalcanal and for Georgia's capital city, *Atlanta* (CL-104) was laid down 25 January 1943. Margaret Mitchell, author of *Gone With The Wind* and sponsor of the cruiser lost off Guadalcanal, returned to the New York City metropolitan area to again christen a light cruiser named *Atlanta*. Launch at New York Shipbuilding Corp.'s Camden, N.J. yard occurred on 6 February 1944 and the new warship was commissioned 3 December 1944 with Capt. B.H. Colyear in command.

War for this *Atlanta* was short. Operating in the Far East for the last four months of war, *Atlanta* screened carriers during the final stages of the Okinawa operation and the last raids against Japan. The cruiser also joined in the bombardment of the Japanese home islands 15-18 July 1945. After a brief period of occupation duty the cruiser continued operations in the Pacific until decommissioned 1 July 1949. Struck from the Navy list 1 October 1962, the cruiser was reinstated in May 1964 as an experimental ship (IX-304). She served in three experimental tests in the Pacific through 1966.

Margaret Mitchell returned to the New York City area on 6 February 1944 to christen the second *Atlanta* (CL-104). Mrs. Mitchell had sponsored the first *Atlanta* (CL-51) three years earlier.   USN

DAYTON CL-105

(1 Battle Star) Named for the city in Ohio, *Dayton* (CL-105) was laid down 8 March 1943 by the New York Shipbuilding Corp. The original hull that was intended to carry the name *Dayton* (CL-78) was converted to the light carrier *Monterey* (CVL-26) on 31 March 1942. *Dayton* (CL-105) was sponsored at her launch 19 March 1944 by Mrs. H. Rueger and was commissioned 7 January 1945 with Capt. P.W. Steinhagan commanding.

Dayton's only combat action was in July and August 1945 when she screened carriers of the Third Fleet during their final strikes on the Japanese home islands and when she trained her guns on targets ashore. On occupation duty until 7 November, the cruiser steamed to California before returning to the Far East in February 1946. Reassigned to the Atlantic Fleet, *Dayton* served in the Mediterranean and off the East Coast of the United States until decommissioned 1 March 1949. The ship was stricken 1 September 1961 and scrapped.

The great, the little-used, and the unused rest and rust together at the Philadelphia Navy Yard 24 August 1961. *Huntington*, which never saw combat, *Dayton* which won only one battle star, and the famous battleship *South Dakota* were all scrapped soon after this photograph was taken.   USN

THE
CRUISER-
CARRIERS (CVLs)

THE CRUISER-CARRIERS (CVLs)

Cruiser-Carriers
Awarded Battle Stars in World War II

CVL-22	*Independence*	8	
CVL-23	*Princeton*	9	
CVL-24	*Belleau Wood*	11	Presidential Unit Citation
CVL-25	*Cowpens*	12	Navy Unit Commendation
CVL-26	*Monterey*	11	
CVL-27	*Langley*	9	Navy Unit Commendation
CVL-28	*Cabot*	9	Presidential Unit Citation
CVL-29	*Bataan**	5	
CVL-30	*San Jacinto*	5	Presidential Unit Citation

*Received 7 Battle Stars for service in Korea.

IT WOULD NOT BE PROPER TO CONCLUDE this survey of the United States Navy's World War II cruisers without a concise overview of the nine cruiser hulls of the *Cleveland* class that were converted to light carriers (CVLs). These nine conversions—officially designated CVLs on 15 July 1943—were not the first American warships laid down as cruisers to be converted to carriers. That distinction belonged to the two big carriers of the *Lexington* class (*Lexington* [CV-2] and *Saratoga* [CV-3]) laid down in 1922 as battlecruisers but completed in 1927 as carriers. Too, the *Cleveland*-class conversions were not the last as two *Baltimore*-class heavy cruiser hulls were converted into the *Saipan*-class light carriers (*Saipan* [CVL-48] and 2 *Wright* [CVL-49]). These last two ships did not receive commissions in time to fight in World War II, but the nine *Independence*-class carriers did not fight and they registered war records as proud as those of any cruiser class.

All nine CVLs won battle stars, which as a group totalled 79. Three (*Belleau Wood, Cabot* and *San Jacinto*) were awarded the Presidential Unit Citation and two (*Langley* and *Cowpens*) received the Navy Unit Commendation. Only *Princeton* was lost due to enemy action (Battle of Leyte Gulf, 24 October 1944 with 108 killed) but three were damaged: *Belleau Wood* was struck by a kamikaze 30 October 1944 off the Philippines and suffered 92 killed; *Independence* was hit by an aerial torpedo off Tarawa 20 November 1943 and counted 17 killed; and *Cabot* lost 36 killed when she was crashed by a kamikaze off Luzon on 25 November 1944.

All nine conversions were completed by the New York Shipbuilding Corp. Since the war was underway as they were being built, emphasis was on getting these "emergency" carriers into the water as soon as possible.

All nine were commissioned in 1943.

The hulls of the *Independence* class were still distinguishable as *Clevelands* even after conversion; the difference of 9 feet in overall length was attributable to the stern anti-aircraft gun mount on the carriers. Beam measurement was 8 feet greater at the water line (71 feet) due to bulges added for stability and storage. Maximum draft was increased by 1 foot to 25 feet. Displacement was up 1,000 tons for the carriers (11,000 standard and 14,300 average war service) and speed was 30 to 31 knots, which allowed the *Independence*-class carriers to operate with the big fleet carriers. Horsepower was 103,000. Each ship had four screws and carried 2,789 tons of oil, which provided a cruising radius of 10,100 miles at 15 knots or 5,800 miles at 25 knots. These radius statistics compared favorably to the *Cleveland*-class cruisers, but were only two-thirds the cruising radius of the *Essex*-class carriers. Complement for these ships was approximately 1,500 men, or 300 more than their *Cleveland*-class cruiser stepsisters.

Although much of the armor protection was omitted from *Independence* and *Princeton*, the other units were protected in a manner similar to their cruiser stepsisters with 3-inch plus 2-inch deck armor and a side belt ranging from 2 to 5 inches. Each carrier was designed to operate up to 45 planes. The 525-foot-long flight deck was served by two elevators and two catapults.

Armament for the *Independence* carriers was light. Although some of the first conversions had a 5-inch gun, they were soon removed in favor of the lighter 40mm guns; the long-range, anti-aircraft gunnery was left to escorts. Usual armament, then, for these carriers was eighteen to twenty-six 40mm barrels and ten to twenty-two 20mm guns.

Only one of the *Independence*-class carriers fought again after World War II. *Bataan* earned 7 battle stars during the Korean War. Still, several units of the class had noteworthy experiences after 1945. *Independence* survived the atomic bomb tests at Bikini in 1946 before being sunk off California in January 1951 in another weapons test. *Belleau Wood* was transferred to France in 1953 for service there, but was returned to the United States, stricken in 1960 and scrapped. *Langley* was also transferred to France in 1951, returned, and sold for scrap in 1963. *Bataan* was sold 1 September 1959, *Cowpens* was stricken 1 November 1959 and scrapped, *San Jacinto* was sold for scrap 15 December 1971 and *Monterey* served as the Navy's training carrier at Pensacola in the early 1950s before being stricken in 1970. *Cabot* still lives at the time of this writing as the helicopter carrier *Dedalo* in Spain.

The feasibility of converting cruiser hulls into carriers had been proven in the 1920s with the conversion of *Lexington* and *Saratoga* (shown here in 1945). USN

San Jacinto in January 1944. Note small island structure and arrangement of stacks. USN

Bataan at Hunters Point 29 September 1944. *Bataan* was the only member of her class to see combat in both World War II and Korea.

USN

Belleau Wood fitting out 27 March 1943, four days before commissioning.   USN

Langley steams ahead of *Ticonderoga* (CV-14), *Washington* (BB-56), *North Carolina* (BB-55), *South Dakota* (BB-57) and three *Cleveland*-class cruisers late in World War II. USN

Close-up of the tremendous damage to *Princeton* just before the explosion that sealed the fate of the carrier and rained death on *Birmingham*. USN

Independence, the class leader, survived a Japanese torpedo off Tarawa in November 1943 and survived the atomic tests in July 1946 (shown here). She was finally sunk off California in another weapons test in 1951. NA

Monterey (right) across the dock from *Enterprise* during the October 1945 Navy Day celebration in New York City. This photograph provides a good perspective on the difference in size of the light carriers and a large carrier.
USN

JAPANESE
CRUISERS

JAPANESE CRUISERS

THE NATURE OF THE WAR IN THE ATLANTIC seemed to promise a major sea battle between German cruisers and those of the United States Navy. But, this promise—or threat—did not materialize. In the Pacific, however, all 45 heavy and light cruisers of the Japanese Navy battled American forces throughout the broad expanse of that great ocean. It is often stated in both Japanese and American histories that the wartime performance of Japanese battleships and submarines was below average, while the performance of aircraft carriers was average, and that the performance of cruisers and destroyers was above average. Certainly it is fair to record here the view that Japanese crews aboard cruisers and destroyers earned the respect of their American counterparts. Indeed, it is fact that in surface actions Japan lost only four cruisers: heavy cruiser *Furutaka* off Cape Esperance 11 October 1942, heavy cruiser *Haguro* sunk by British destroyers in the Malacca Straits 15-16 May 1945, light cruiser *Jintsu* at Kolombangara 13 July 1943, and light cruiser *Sendai* at Empress Augusta Bay 2 November 1943. The U.S. Navy, in contrast, lost seven (five heavy cruisers and two light cruisers).

By the end of World War II, Japan had lost 40 of 45 cruisers. In 1942 six cruisers were lost and in 1943 only two were sunk, but 24 were lost in 1944 and eight more went under in 1945 (three during the July 1945 raids on Kure). Fifteen Japanese cruisers were sunk by submarines (two by British subs, the other 13 by United States subs), 15 were lost by aerial action, six were lost by a combination of surface and aerial action and four, as mentioned, were lost in surface actions. Of Japanese heavy cruisers only *Myoko* and *Takao* survived the war; the 16 lost included four by submarines, two in surface actions, six by planes and four lost in combined surface-air actions. Three light cruisers survived the war: *Kashima*, *Kitakami*, and *Sakawa*, which was expended in the atom bomb tests at Bikini in 1946. The 24 light cruisers lost included 11 sunk by submarines, two in surface actions, nine by planes and two in combined surface-air actions.

To generalize, at the beginning of the war Japanese cruisers were a little older (and more experienced) than American cruisers. Too, they were more powerful (up to 152,000 horsepower in some units), slightly faster, heavier, and they carried a heavier punch thanks to retention of above-water torpedo tubes. But these cruisers were not as well armored as American cruisers and they did not have as great a cruising range.

One of only two Japanese heavy cruisers to survive World War II, *Myoko* is seen here anchored at Shanghai, China, 16 August 1934.   USN

Mikuma sinking during the June 1942 Battle of Midway. *Mikuma's* troubles began when she collided with sister ship *Mogami* and she was finished by planes from *Enterprise* and *Hornet*. *Mikuma* was one of the cruisers that had fatally damaged *Houston* (CA-30) in the Battle of the Java Sea.
USN

Japanese sailors transfer Admiral Ozawa's headquarters from the sinking carrier *Zuikaku* to the light cruiser *Oyodo* during the Battle off Cape Engano 25 October 1944. *Oyodo* was sunk at Kure 28 July 1945 by Navy planes.
USN

Twenty-one of the 40 Japanese cruisers lost during World War II were sunk by planes or by a combination of air-surface action.
USN

-132-

CRUISER
SCOUT
OBSERVATION
PLANES

CRUISER SCOUT OBSERVATION PLANES

EXCEPT FOR THE *ATLANTA-OAKLAND* CLASS, the cruisers that fought in World War II carried from one to four scout-observation planes. Some of the cruisers had the capability of carrying up to eight aircraft, but the norm was three to four planes. Throughout the literature of the era these planes were referred to as "float planes," "spotter planes," "scout planes" and by other less-used terms.

Throughout the mid 1930s the Vought 03U Corsair biplane was the standard cruiser-borne aircraft. In the late 1930s and early into the war the standard plane was the Curtiss SOC Seagull. Four different versions of this biplane saw service and many were still in service at the end of the war. Cruisers reporting for duty later in the war usually carried the OS2U Vought Kingfisher, a low-wing monoplane with a top speed of 164 mph.

Flying from a cruiser was dangerous work, just as it was from a carrier. But a carrier pilot did have the advantage of returning to a solid deck. When the cruiser pilot returned from his usually thankless and non-glorious flight, he first had to find his ship, which quite often was not where he expected to find it, then he had to wait for his cruiser to make a sharp turn to knock down the top of the waves and create a slick in the lee of the ship. Landings were still a controlled crash similar to landing on a carrier. Then the pilot had to taxi in the open sea to catch the ship, taxi onto a sled, and cut the engine and engage a hook from the cruiser's crane onto a ring at the top of the wing. The plane would then be lifted aboard while the cruiser continued to steam at 3 to 6 knots.

The above procedure appears to be relatively simple, functional and routine. However, conversation with former cruiser pilots is punctuated with stories about a multitude of occasions when getting back on board was anything but simple. Strong winds often caused a pilot not to find his ship at "point option" and therefore an "expanding search" or "square search" was necessary. This pattern of flying consisted of flying first into the wind for 10 miles, then turning 90 degrees and flying for 20 miles, then another 90 degree turn for 30 miles and so on until fuel was consumed. Nor were one's worries over once the cruiser was located. After landing, a pilot would often lose sight of his ship due to high waves. Then there was always a possibility of slamming against the side of the ship when approaching the sled. Ideally, the connection of the cable from the ship's crane to the ring on the plane would be completed by the radio operator-gunner in the rear seat. If the hook broke, or if the radio operator was hoisted out of the plane by an over-anxious crane operator (which is what happened to an acquaintance of this writer), the American taxpayers lost a plane and the pilot would be fished out of the ocean by a destroyer.

The SOC Seagull was a dependable plane despite its less-than impressive performance statistics. Wide open, the Seagull was capable of only 150 miles per hour (this is the Navy's figure; Cmdr. Perry Ustick says 150 mph was possible only in a fatal crash dive). Fuel capacity was 90 gallons for a range of approximately 800 miles. Usual time in the air, however, was four hours. Armament consisted of one fixed .30-caliber machine gun forward, one "free" mounted machine gun in the rear cockpit and 200 pounds of bombs.

A carrier pilot was considered a "fighter" regardless whether he flew a bomber, torpedo plane or fighter aircraft. The cruiser pilot, with his back-seat crew member, was primarily an observer for the accuracy of the ship's main armament gunfire, a hunter of submarines, a scout for the fleet and a rescuer of downed pilots in combat zones. However, on the first day of World War II for the United States, 7 December 1941, radio operator-gunner Robert Baxter in a Seagull from *Northampton* was credited with downing a Japanese Zero with his .30-caliber flexible machine gun. The action report, now in the National Archives, does mention the obvious fact that the Japanese pilot did not have sufficient respect for the Seagull.

An 025U Vought Kingfisher on the battleship *Alabama* in Mobile. The Kingfisher flew from cruisers in the latter stages of the war.

Courtesy of Larry J. Early

A Vought Corsair is catapulted off *Augusta* in 1935. Speeds of 70 mph could be attained over the 60- to 70-foot catapults.
USN

SOC-1's from *Northampton* flying over Hawaii just prior to World War II. These Seagulls were active on cruisers throughout the war.
Courtesy of Cmdr. Perry W. Ustick

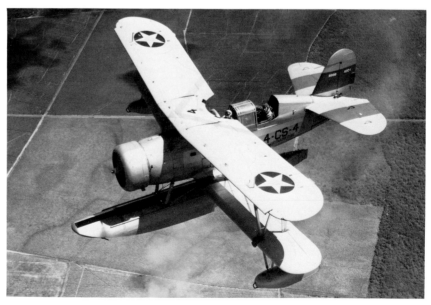